# Nordic Felted Knits

# Nordic Felted Knits

SEARCH PRESS

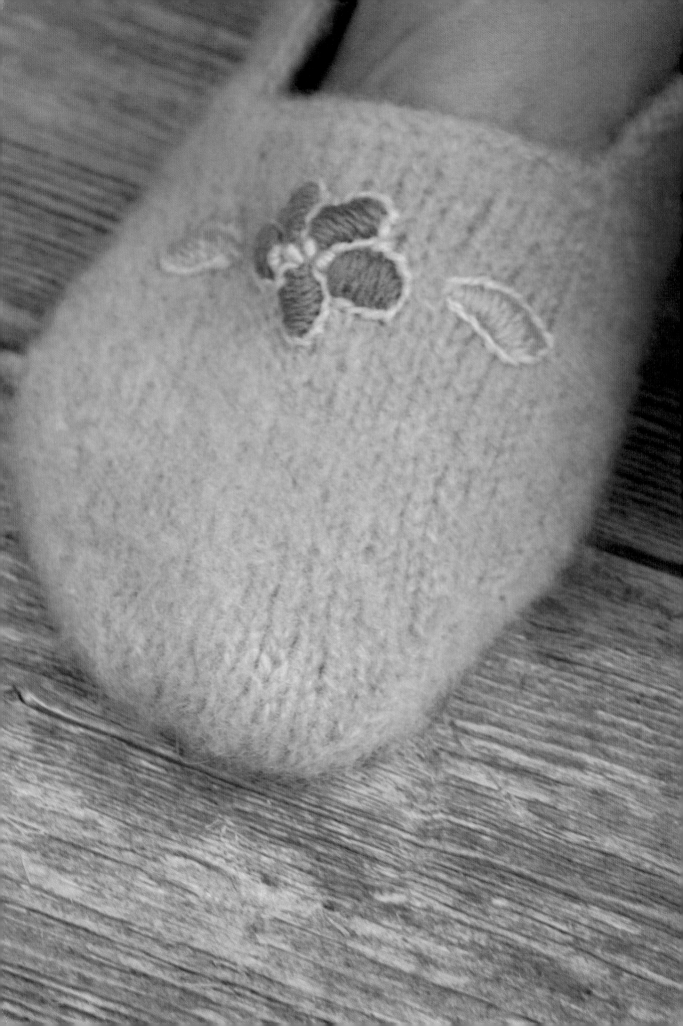

# Foreword

Knitting is a hobby that has much to recommend it. Many people find it relaxing, it gives you an outlet for your creativity and all you need to get started is two hands, a ball of wool and a set of knitting needles.

Felting adds a new, exciting dimension to this hobby. It produces warm, soft, hard-wearing, very user-friendly articles. Furthermore, the smooth, fleecy surface makes a good basis for trimming with embroidery and beadwork.

In this book you will find patterns for everyday and evening bags, pretty sweaters and small garments to keep you warm on chilly days. We show you patterns for a lovely crochet rug and a soft, fleecy cushion. You will also find the sweetest angel in the world and one or two goodies for Christmas and Easter.

Most of the designs are relatively quick and easy to knit and very suitable for beginners. For more experienced readers, they offer a basis for experimenting with colours and patterns.

If our choice of colours doesn't suit your taste or your wardrobe, wool shops will have a variety of fashionable colours to choose from.

Knit for yourself or for someone you care about. You can make great gifts for your friends and family. Get out your knitting needles and get started!

Good luck!

*Gjerd Fjellanger*

Gjerd Fjellanger
Editor and designer

# Notes

The instructions in this book suggest circular needles, or sets of 5 double-pointed needles, as used in Europe, rather than 4, as commonly sold in the UK. The sizes given are metric. The old UK equivalents for sizes used in this book are:

| Metric: | 3.5mm | 4mm | 4.5mm | 5mm | 6mm | 6.5mm | 8mm |
|---------|-------|-----|-------|-----|-----|-------|-----|
| Old UK: | 9 | 8 | 7 | 6 | 4 | 3 | 0 |
| US: | | 4 | 6 | 7 | 8 | 10 | – | 11 |

The recommended yarns come in 50g balls. In this book, articles or parts of articles are sometimes worked in rows backwards and forwards on the circular needle instead of in rounds. This is indicated by the instruction 'work in rows' or 'work in rounds'. Stocking stitch is worked by knitting 1 row plain, 1 row purl in rows and every round plain in the round. Garter stitch is worked by knitting every row plain when working in rows, and 1 round plain, 1 round purl when working in rounds. When articles are knitted in garter stitch, this book often counts in 'ridges' rather than rows. A ridge is formed by working 2 rows/rounds in garter stitch as described above.

# Abbreviations

st(s) = stitch(es)
s = slip
k = knit
p = purl
yfd = yarn forward
k2tog = knit 2 together
k2togtbl = knit 2 together through back of loops
s1, k1, psso = slip 1, knit 1, pass slipped stitch over
rh = right hand
lh = left hand

*...* = repeat from * to *
beg = begin, beginning
rd(s) = round(s)
rep = repeat
st st = stocking stitch
crochet:
ch = chain
ss = slip stitch/single crochet
dc = double crochet
tr = treble crochet

# Contents

# Felting

The results of felting vary from one washing machine to another and depend on the quantity and size of the pieces to be felted. A single small piece will end up smaller than several small pieces or one large item. The tension of the knitting will also have a part to play.

## How to felt knitted items in the washing machine:

We recommend using a liquid non-biological detergent. Pure soft soap or Woolite give the best results. Felt the item at 40°C. Use a gentle or short wash programme with a full spin. Stretch and shape the work after washing so it ends up the right size. When you wash it later, you should treat it like an ordinary woollen item.

If the work is not sufficiently felted, repeat the process. On the other hand, if the work has felted too much, you can try to rescue it by rinsing it with hair conditioner and then stretching it well. You can repeat this several times during the drying process. You can also use an iron when stretching it.

## Suitable yarn for felting:

To obtain the desired effect, you should use the type of woollen yarn called 'kardegarn' (carded wool). You should not use 'kamgarn' (combed wool) for the patterns in this book. Bleached yarn, or yarn marked 'superwash', is not suitable for felting. Sometimes different colours give different results.

# Triangular shawl, hat and bag

This pretty shawl is easy to knit, though the hole pattern around the edge needs a little practice.
The shawl is knitted in garter stitch and the patterned border is added afterwards.
The bag is also knitted in garter stitch and edged with the same border.
A hatband is inserted around the crown of the hat so that it will keep its shape and sit properly.

**Yarn:**
**Røros Lamullgarn:**
Turquoise L70          5 balls
**Rauma Finullgarn:**
Brown 411               3 balls

**65 cm hatband**

**Suggestions for trimming:**
**Hat:** 90 cm (36 in) x 1.5 cm (⅝ in) turquoise velvet ribbon, 1 large 1 cm (⅜ in) mother-of-pearl faceted bead, small shiny beads
**Bag:** Large metal beads

**Measurements:** After felting, the shawl measures approximately 170 cm (67½ in) and the bag about 30 x 25 cm (12 x 10 in). The hat should be shaped to the desired size.

**Suggested needles:** Circular needles size 4 mm and 5 mm and crochet hook size 3 mm
**Tension for Røros Lamullgarn:**
**Before felting:** Approx 17 sts garter st = 10 cm (4 in)
**After felting:** Approx 20 sts = 10 cm (4 in)
**Tension for Rauma Finullgarn:**
**Before felting:** Approx 14 sts garter st = 10 cm (4 in)
**After felting:** Approx 18 sts = 10 cm (4 in)
**Before felting:** Approx 16 sts st st = 10 cm (4 in)
**After felting:** Approx 20 sts = 10 cm (4 in)

## Triangular shawl:

With 4 mm circular needle and turquoise yarn, cast on 439 sts. Work in garter stitch in rows, decreasing 1 st at each end and 1 st on either side of the centre stitch on alternate rows until all the stitches have been cast off. Make the lace edging as follows: with

4 mm circular needle and turquoise yarn, cast on 14 sts.
**Rows 1 and 3:** S1, k1, yfd, k2togtbl (= s1, k1, psso), yfd, k1, k2togtbl, p1, k2tog, k1, yfd, k3.
**Rows 2 and 4:** s1, p5, k1, p5, k2.
**Row 5:** S1, k1, yfd, k2togtbl, yfd, k1, yfd, k2togtbl, p1, k2tog, yfd, k4.
**Row 6:** S1, p5, k1, p6, k2.
**Row 7:** S1, k1, yfd, k2togtbl, yfd, k3, yfd, k3tog, yfd, k5.
**Row 8:** S1, k1, p13, k2.
**Row 9:** S1, k1, yfd, k2togtbl, yfd, k5, yfd, k7.
**Row 10:** Cast off 4 st (= 1 st remaining on rh needle), p11, k2 (= 14 st on needle).
These 10 rows form the pattern repeat. Knit 2 lace borders, each measuring approx 110 cm (43½ in). (To be on the safe side, measure the short sides of the shawl and add 5 cm (2½ in).) End with the last row of a pattern. Sew the lace borders to the edges of the shawl and sew together at the bottom of the point.
Felt as described on page 8, but at 30°C. Use a very gentle wash programme.

## Bag:

With 5 mm circular needle and brown yarn, cast on 100 sts. Work in garter stitch in rows. Knit 55 rows and cast off loosely. Fold in two and sew the sides together. Pick up 110 sts along the top edge by working 1 stitch into the end stitch of each ridge. Work the hole pattern by repeating *k2tog, yfd* over the whole round. Work 1 rd p and 1 rd k until 4 ridges have been formed. Cast off loosely. Make the lace edging as follows: with 4 mm circular needle and turquoise yarn, cast on 22 sts.
**Row 1:** S1, k9, yfd, k2togtbl (= s1, k1, psso), yfd, k1, k2togtbl, p1, k2tog, k1, yfd, k3.

**Row 2:** S1, p5, k1, p5, k10.
**Row 3:** S1, k5, yfd, k2tog, k2, yfd, k2togtbl, yfd, k1, k2togtbl, p1, k2tog, k1, yfd, k3.
**Row 4:** S1, p5, k1, p5, k10.
**Row 5:** S1, k9, yfd, k2togtbl, yfd, k1, yfd, p1, k2togtbl, p1, k2tog, yfd, k4.
**Row 6:** S1, p5, k1, p5, k10.
**Row 7:** S1, k5, yfd, k2tog, k2, yfd, k2togtbl, yfd, k3, yfd, k3tog, yfd, k5.
**Row 8:** S1, p13, k10.
**Row 9:** S1, k9, yfd, k2togtbl, yfd, k5, yfd, k7.
**Row 10:** Cast off 4 st (= 1 st remaining on rh needle), p11, k10 (= 22 sts on needle).
**Row 11:** S1, k5, yfd, k2tog, k2, yfd, k2togtbl, yfd, k1, k2togtbl, p1, k2tog, k1, yfd, k3.
**Row 12:** S1, p5, k1, p5, k10.
**Row 13:** S1, k9, yfd, k2togtbl, yfd, k1, k2togtbl, p1, k2tog, k1, yfd, k3.
**Row 14:** S1, p5, k1, p5, k10.
**Row 15:** S1, k5, s1, k2tog, k2, yfd, k2togtbl, yfd, k1, yfd, k2togtbl, p1, k2tog, yfd, k4.
**Row 16:** S1, p5, k1, p6, k10.
**Row 17:** S1, k9, yfd, k2togtbl, yfd, k3, yfd, k3tog, yfd, k5.
**Row 18:** S1, p13, k10.

**Row 19:** S1, k5, yfd, k2tog, k2, yfd, k2togtbl, yfd, k5, yfd, k7.

**Row 20:** Cast off 4 sts (= 1 st remaining on rh needle), p11, k10 (= 22 sts on needle).

Repeat rows 1–20 until you have worked 55 holes in the garter stitch edge (the outermost holes should have 3 rows between them). Cast off loosely. Sew the ends together.

Felt the components as described on page 8.

Make a cord approx 90 cm (36 in) long of brown yarn (used double). Position the lace edging around the bag, matching the edges at the top, and thread the cord through the rows of holes on the lace and the bag.

To make the handles, thread beads on double yarn. Fasten the ends of the strands to the inside of the bag, just above the row of holes and about 7 cm (2¾ in) in from the sides.

Pull the cord gently so the bag is nicely gathered, and tie a bow at one side. If desired, attach a bead to each end of the cord.

## Hat:

With 5 mm circular needle and brown yarn, cast on 180 sts. Work 4 rds st st. Round 5: decrease on by working *k7, k2tog* to end of round. Work 4 rounds. Next round: decrease by working *k6, k2tog* to end of round. Work 4 rounds. Next round: *k5, k2tog* to end of round. Work 4 rounds. Next round: *k4, k2tog* to end of round = 100 sts. Work 28 rounds straight. Decrease on next round by working *k8, k2tog* to end of round. Work 2 rounds. Next round: decrease by working *k7, k2tog* to end of round. Continue decreasing like this on every 3rd round with 1 less st between decreases each time until 10 sts remain. Cut the yarn and pull it through the stitches.

Felt as described on page 8.

Mark the round after the last decrease of the brim with a tacking thread. Measure round your head and add 3 cm (1¼ in) to give you the length of the hatband. Sew the ends of the hatband together with a 1.5 cm (⅝ in)

seam. Press the seam open. Pin the band to the inside of the hat, just above the tacking thread. Tack it in place, then sew it in with small stitches along the top and bottom. Sew the decorative ribbon to the outside in the same way.

Using turquoise yarn, crochet a **medium rosette** as described on page 13.

Make a small rosette of velvet ribbon. Using double thread, sew a hem along one edge and pull tight. Sew small beads close together along the outer edge. Sew a bead in the centre of the rosette. Attach the rosette to the crochet rosette and sew them firmly on to the hat.

# Girl's hat with rosette

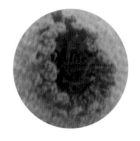

Get out your knitting needles — you can knit this hat in one evening.

**Sizes:** 2/4 – 6/8 – 10/12 years

**Yarn: Rauma Finullgarn** (or **pt2**):

Green 455 (15)     1 ball
Lime 454 (16)     1 ball
Pink 465 (54)     1 ball

**Suggestions for trimming:**
One large red satin rose (or several small ones)

**Measurements:** Shape the hat by trying on or by measuring the head.

**Suggested needles:** Short circular needle 40cm (16in), set of 5 double-pointed needles and crochet hook size 5 mm

**Tension:**
**Before felting:** Approx 16 sts st st = 10 cm (4 in)
**After felting:** Approx 20 sts = 10 cm (4 in)

With green yarn, cast on 78 – 84 – 90 sts. Work in st st in rounds in alternate stripes of 1 rd lime and 1 rd green. Work 26 – 31 – 36 rounds. Next round: decrease 8 – 4 – 0 sts, evenly spaced = 70 – 80 – 90 sts. Work 2 rounds without decreasing. Next round: *k5 – 6 – 7, k2tog* to end of round. Work 2 rds straight. Next round: *k4 – 5 – 6, k2tog* to end of round. Continue decreasing in the same way on every 3rd round, with 1 less st between decreases each time, until 10 sts remain. Cut the yarn and pull it through the stitches. Fasten off. With pink yarn, crochet around the cast-on edge as follows: 1dc in first st, 3 ch, 1 dc in first ch (picot), *miss 1 st, 1 dc in next st, 1 picot*, repeat from * to * and finish with 1 ss in first dc.
Felt as described on page 8

## Rosette:

With pink yarn, crochet 7 ch, ss in first ch to form a ring.
**Round 1:** 2ch (= first tr), work 14 more tr in ring, finish with 1ss in first tr.

**Round 2:** 1ch (= first dc) 2dc in next tr, *1dc in next tr, 2dc in next tr*, repeat from * to * = 23 dc, finish with 1ss in first dc.
**Round 3:** 8ch, *1dc in next st, 8ch* repeat from * to * and finish with 1ss in first dc. Sew the satin rose in the centre of the rosette and attach the rosette to the hat approx 3 cm (1¼ in) from the edge.

# Embroidered bag

Choose your own favourite colours for this bag. If you want it to be simpler and less time-consuming, you can choose one of the motifs and embroider it in the middle of the bag.

**Yarn: pt2**

| | |
|---|---|
| Red 59 | 2 balls |
| Burgundy 51 | 1 ball |
| Pink 54 | 1 ball |
| Orange 70 | 1 ball |
| Lime 16 | 1 ball |
| Green 10 | 1 ball |

**Measurements:** After felting, the bag measures approx 25 x 27cm (10 x 10¾ in).

**Suggested needles:** Short circular needle 40cm (16in) and crochet hook size 5mm

**Tension:**
**Before felting:** Approx 16 sts st st = 10cm (4 in)
**After felting:** Approx 20 sts = 10cm (4 in)

With red yarn, cast on 100 st. Work 100 rounds in st st. Cast off.
**Handles:** With red yarn, crochet 155 ch. Work ss along one side of the chain and then along the other side as follows. 1 ss in 3rd ch from hook and in every following ch, turn, 1 ch, 1 ss in

2nd ch and every following ch. Make 2 handles the same.

Felt the bag and the handles as described on page 8.

Attach the handles to the bag approx 5 cm (2 in) from the sides.

Embroider the motifs as shown in the sketches.

Sew the bag together along the bottom.

Solid lines = stem stitch

5 French knots with thread wrapped round 5 times

French knots with thread wrapped round twice

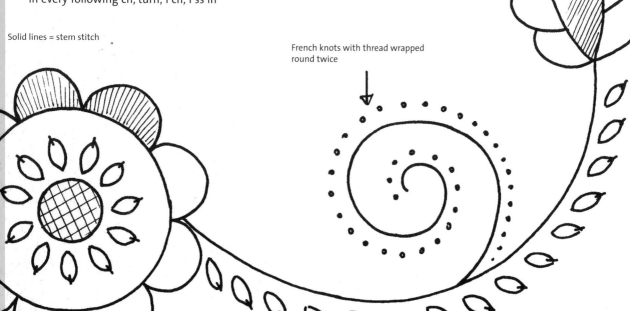

# Patterned bag

This pretty bag with its simple hole pattern is quick to knit in thick yarn on big needles.

**Yarn: Rauma Vamsegarn:**
Green V81          4 balls

**Suggestions for trimming:** 8 mm pastel green beads

**Measurements:** After felting, the bag measures approx 29 x 29 cm (11½ x 11½ in)

**Suggested needles:** Short circular needle 40cm (16in) size 8 mm

**Tension:**
**Before felting:** Approx 10 sts hole pattern = 10 cm (4 in)
**After felting:** Approx 14 sts = 10 cm (4 in)

Cast on 90 st. K3 rds st st. Work the pattern from the chart in rounds. Work the pattern repeat 3 times (60 rows). Then k1 rd, decreasing 10 sts evenly over the round. Work 4 rds. Work 1 rd purl to mark the edge of the fold, then 4 rounds st st. Cast off. Fold the top edge over to the wrong side and sew down. Sew together along the bottom and 5cm (2in) along the top at each side. Sew on beads.
**Handles:** Cast on 60 st. Work 8 rows st st. Cast off. Sew the cast-on and cast-off edges together. Make 2 handles the same. Sew the handles firmly to the bag about 10 cm (4 in) from each side.
Felt as described on page 8.

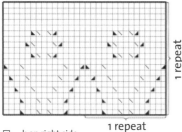

1 repeat

□ = k on right side,
      p on wrong side

◲ = yfd

◪ = k2tog

◤ = s1, k1, psso

# Fancy bag

This bag is worked using double yarn, pt2 or Rauma Finullgarn and Rio. Rio is a fancy yarn that comes in twenty different colours. Put your favourite colours together.

**Yarn: pt2** (or **Rauma Finullgarn**) and **Rio:**
Green 15 (455)      1 ball
Green Rio 1811      2 balls

**For this bag you will need two handles in wood or plastic with an outer circumference of about 48 cm (19 in)**

**Measurements:** After felting, the bag measures approx 25 x 22 cm (10 x 8¾ in).

**Suggested needles:** Short circular needles 40cm (16in) size 5 mm

**Tension:**
**Before felting:** Approx 16 sts st st = 10 cm (4 in)
**After felting:** Approx 20 sts = 10 cm (4 in)

Using wool and Rio together, cast on 100 sts. Work 65 rds in st st. Divide the work into 2 sets of 50 sts and complete each side separately. Work 15 rows st st. Continue using wool only. *K2tog* to end of row = 25 sts. Leave sts on needle.
**Handle:** Cast on 65 sts at beg of rd = 90 sts. Work 15 rds. Cast off. Complete the other side to match.
Felt as described on page 8.
Position the knitted handles around the bought handles and sew together. Sew the bottom of the bag together.

# Hat and mittens with embroidered rose
# Striped scarf

The hat and gloves are worked in stocking stitch and have a ribbed border. The borders and the flowers are embroidered in chain stitch before the articles are felted. The scarf is knitted in garter stitch.

**Sizes:** XS/S – M/L

**Yarn:** pt2 (or **Rauma Finullgarn**)

**Colour 1:** Dark green 21 (432)          3 balls
**Colour 2:** Grey 84 (405)          1 ball
**Colour 3:** Light grey 82 (403)          1 ball
**Colour 4:** Bright green 15 (455)          1 ball
**Colour 5:** Yellow-green 11 (498)          1 ball
**Colour 6:** Warm green 10 (489)          1 ball
**Colour 7:** Pink 54 (465)          1 ball
**Colour 8:** Pale pink 55 (479)          1 ball
**Colour 9:** Red 52 (456)          1 ball
**Colour 10:** Dark red 51 (499)          1 ball

**Suggested needles:** Short circular needle 40cm (16in) and set of 5 short double-pointed needles size 5mm
Set of 5 short double-pointed needles size 4.5mm

**Tension before felting (on 5mm needles):**
Approx 16 sts = 10 cm (4 in)

**Tension after felting:**
Approx 20 sts = 10 cm (4 in)

## Hat:

With colour 3 and circular needle, cast on 96 sts. Work 1 rd in k2, p2 rib. Change to colour 2 and work 6 in rib. Change to colour 1 and work in st st until the work measures approx 22cm (9in), decreasing 6 sts evenly spaced on the last round. Work 2 rds st st. Next round *k 7, k2tog* repeat to end of round. Work 2 rounds. Next round: *k6, k2tog* to end of rd. Continue decreasing on every 3rd rd, with 1 less st between decreases each time, until 5 decreases have been worked. Then decrease on every alternate rd twice (= 20 sts). Cut the yarn and pull it through the stitches. Using chain stitch, embroider the motif as shown in section A of the chart just above the ribbed border all the way round. Then embroider section B.

## Mittens:

With colour 3 and set of 4.5mm double-pointed needles, cast on 40 sts and place 10 on each needle. Work 1 round in k2, p2 rib. Change to colour 2 and work 6 rounds in rib. Change to 5mm needles and colour 1 and work in st st. When the work measures approx 11cm (4½in), knit with a marker thread of a different colour over the first 7 sts of the round for the thumb. Slip these 7 sts back onto the lh needle. Continue in rounds until work measures approx 25cm (10in). Place markers on each side, at the start of the round and after 20 sts. Decrease 1 st on either side of the markers on every alternate rd 6 times (= 15 sts). Graft together.

**Thumb:** Remove the marker thread and slip the stitches on to 4 needles. Knit up 1 st at each side (= 16 sts). Work 8cm st st. Then k2tog until 4 sts remain. Cut off yarn and pull it through the stitches. For the second mitten, work the thumb over the last 7 stitches of the round. Embroider the motif shown in section A of the chart just above the ribbed border all the way round. Embroider section B approx 8 cm (3¼ in) from the cast-on edge.

## Scarf:

With 5mm needle and colour 2, cast on 30 sts. Work in rows in garter stitch. Work 7 rows in each colour in the following sequence: colours 2, 4, 8, 7, 10, 6, 3, 5, 9. Repeat until scarf measures approx 260cm (102 in) – approx 2m (79 in) after felting.

Felt the articles as described on page 8.

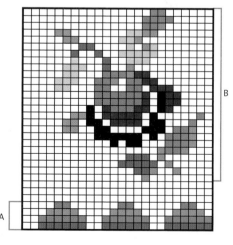

# Two-tone bag

The bag is worked in rounds in stocking stitch. The strap is knitted in rows in garter stitch and sewn on at the end. Decorate with a velvet ribbon and a crochet rosette. Choose colours to suit your wardrobe.

**Yarn: Rauma Finullgarn**

| | |
|---|---|
| Green 476 | 2 balls |
| Pink 473 | 1 ball |
| Light green 489 | 1 ball |

**Suggestions for trimming:**
60 cm (24 in) pink velvet ribbon, pale pink satin flower, pink sequins and small, shiny beads

**Measurements:** After felting, the bag measures approx 25 x 28 cm (10 x 11 in) (measured inside the strap)

**Suggested needles:** Circular needle size 5 mm and 2 short needles size 4.5 mm

**Tension:**

**Before felting:** Approx 16 sts st st = 10 cm (4 in)
**After felting:** Approx 20 sts = 10 cm (4 in)

With green yarn and 5 mm circular needle, cast on 100 sts. Work 70 rds st st. Change to pink and work a further 30 rds. Cast off. Sew together at the bottom.
**Strap:** With green and 4.5 mm needles, cast on 10 sts. Work approx 200 cm (79 in) in garter st in rows. Cast off.
Felt the parts as described on page 8. Sew the strap along the sides of the bag. Sew on the ribbon so it covers the change of colour. With light green yarn, crochet a large rosette, see below. Sew

sequins and beads just inside the ch st loops (push the needle up through the sequin, through a small bead and back down through the sequin). Sew the flower firmly in the centre of the rosette. Position the rosette in the middle of the ribbon and sew it on firmly.

## Large rosette:

Work 7 ch, ss in first ch to form a ring.
**Round 1:** 2 ch (= 1 tr), work 14 more tr in ring, finish with 1 ss in first tr.
**Round 2:** 2 ch (= 1tr) 2tr in each tr = 30 tr, finish with 1 ss in first tr.
**Round 3:** 1 dc in first st, 9 ch, *1 dc in next st, 9 ch*, repeat from * to * and finish with 1 ss in first dc.

# Hat and mittens in double yarn

These take very little time to knit in stocking stitch using double yarn on big needles.

**Size:** Men's

**Røros Lamullgarn:**

Grey L13          2 balls
Light grey L12    2 balls

**Measurements:** Shape the mittens to fit the hand. Shape the hat by trying it on or measuring round the head.

**Suggested needles:** Short circular needle 40cm (16in) and set of 5 double-pointed needles size 6 mm

**Tension:**

**Before felting:** Approx 12 sts st st = 10 cm (4 in)

**After felting:** Approx 16 st = 10 cm (4 in)

## Hat:

Using circular needle and 1 strand of each colour together, cast on 85 sts. Work 25 rds st st. Decrease 5 sts evenly on next rd. Work 2 rds. Decrease on the next round by working *k6, k2tog* rep to end. Work 2 rds. Decrease by working *k5, k2tog*, rep to end of rd. Continue decreasing on every 3rd round, working 1 less st between decreases each time, until 10 sts remain. Fasten off. Cut the yarn and pull it through the stitches.

## Mittens:

Using circular needle and 1 strand of each colour together, cast on 34 sts. Work 10 rds in st st, increasing 4 sts evenly on the last rd. Continue in rounds until the work measures 16 cm (6½ in). For the thumb, knit the first 7 sts of the round with a marker thread of a different colour. Slip these 7 sts back onto the lh needle. Continue in rounds until work measures approx 30 cm (12 in). Place a marker at each side, at the beginning of the round and after 19 sts. Cast off 1 st on either side of the markers on every other round 6 times (= 14 sts). Graft together.

**Thumb:** Remove the marker thread and slip the stitches on to 4 needles. Pick up and knit 1 st at each side (= 15 sts). Work 8 cm st st. Then k2tog until 4 sts remain. Cut off yarn and pull it through the stitches.

For the second mitten, work the thumb over the last 7 stitches of the round. Felt as described on page 8.

# Striped scarf and winter bag

The scarf is worked lengthways in garter stitch with two rows in each colour. The bag is worked as a single long piece of stocking stitch and sewn together around the strap with the stitching visible on the outside. If the bag is to be used to carry heavy things like books, both the bag and the strap should be lined.

**Yarn: Rauma Finullgarn**

| Charcoal grey 414 | 4 balls |
|---|---|
| Light grey 403 | 1 ball |
| Dark blue 438 | 1 ball |
| Blue 451 | 1 ball |
| Orange 461 | 1 ball |

**Measurements:** After felting, the bag measures approx 30 x 30 cm (12 x 12 in)
The scarf measures approx 120 cm (47 in)
**Suggested needles:** Circular needle size 5 mm
**Tension:**
**Before felting:** Approx 16 sts st st = 10 cm (4 in)
**After felting:** Approx 20 sts = 10 cm (4 in)

## Bag:

With charcoal grey, cast on 60 sts. Work 120 cm (47 in) st st in rows. Cast off.
**Strap:** with charcoal grey, cast on 12 sts. Work 225 cm (88 in) st st in rows. Cast off.
Felt as described on page 8.
Fold bag as shown. Sew the edges of the strap to the sides of the bag as illustrated. Sew from the right side, about 0.5 cm (¼ in) in from the edge. Embroider the snowflake in the centre of the flap.

## Scarf:

With blue yarn, cast on 260 sts. Work in rows of garter stitch throughout. K 1 row. Change to orange and work 2 rows. Work in stripes, knitting 2 rows in each colour in the following sequence: light grey, charcoal grey, blue, orange, dark blue, light grey, charcoal grey, blue, orange, dark blue, light grey = centre stripe. Continue with the stripes in reverse order so they form a mirror image around the centre stripe. Cast off.

Felt as described on page 4. Cut strands 25 cm (10 in) long for the fringes in all of the colours (finished tassles are approximately 12 cm – 4¾ in long). Each tassle consists of a single strand. Knot a tassel through each ridge of the same colour.

# Turquoise bag and hat

The hat is an elegant shape and fits well. Both the bag and the hat are very easy to knit. The matching fabric on the top, decorative beadwork and crochet rosette give the bag a touch of stylish individuality.

**Yarn:** Rauma Finullgarn (or **pt2**): Turquoise 483 (27)   3 balls

**Suggestions for trimming:**
10 cm (4 in) matching fabric. 1 x 10 mm and about 12 x 5–6 mm faceted pearlised beads. Turquoise sequins and small shiny beads. Turquoise faceted beads (approx 4 mm) and 3 leaf-shaped beads or sequins. About 46 turquoise 10 mm faceted beads for the handles.

**Measurements:** After felting, the bag measures approx 32 x 26 cm (12¾ x 10¼ in)

**Suggested needles:** Short circular needle 40 cm (16 in) size 5 mm

**Tension:**
**Before felting:** Approx 16 sts st st = 10 cm (4 in)
**After felting:** Approx 20 sts = 10 cm (4 in)

## Bag:

Cast on 120 sts. Work 60 rds st st. Next round: k2tog to end of rd, halving the number of sts. Work a further 28 rds. Cast off. Sew together along the bottom. Felt as described on page 8.

Measure the width of the bag and the height between the decrease round and the top. Cut fabric to these measurements, adding 1 cm (⅜ in) along the bottom and side edges and 2–3 cm (⅞ – 1¼ in) along the top edge. Sew the short ends together. With right sides together, sew (preferably by hand) the bottom edge of the fabric along the line of decreasing. Turn in the top edge and sew down. Sew sequins and beads along the line where the knitting and fabric meet (attach each sequin with a bead by passing the needle up through the sequin, through the bead and back down through the sequin).

Crochet a **large rosette** as described on page 20. Sew sequins and beads just

inside the ch st loops. Sew the large bead in the centre and the smaller beads in a circle around it. String about 25 beads, alternating shiny and turquoise beads, on a thread, with the leaf-shaped bead at the end. Pass the thread back through the beads and make a good knot. Make 3 strings of beads in this way and attach them to the back of the rosette. Sew the rosette firmly to the bag (see photo).

**Handle:** String the large turquoise beads on a strong thread (e.g. beading thread or waxed linen thread). Fasten the final bead firmly at each end. Make two handles the same and attach them to the bag, about 4 cm (1⅝ in) from the sides.

## Hat:

Cast on 180 sts. Work 4 rds in st st. Round 5: decrease by working *k7, k2tog*, rep to end. Work 4 rds. Next round: decrease by working *k6, k2tog* rep to end. Work 4 rds. Next round: *k5, k2tog*

rep to end. Work 4 rds. Next round: *k4, k2tog* rep to end = 100 sts. Work 28 rds. Next round: decrease by working *k8, k2tog* rep to end. Work 2 rds. Next round: *k7, k2tog* rep to end. Continue decreasing in the same way on every 3rd round, with 1 stitch less between decreases each time until 10 sts remain. Cut the yarn and pull through sts. Felt as described on page 4. Mark the round after the last decrease for the brim with a tacking thread. Measure round your head and add 3 cm (1⅜ in) to give you the length of the hatband. Sew the ends of the hatband together with a 1.5 cm (⅝ in) seam. Press the seam open. Pin it to the inside of the hat, just above the tacking thread. Tack it firmly in place, then sew along the top and bottom edges with small stitches.

To decorate, you could sew on small satin flowers (see photo) or crochet a rosette and decorate it as described for the bag, but without the strings of beads at the back. Attach the rosette on a level with the hatband.

# Cozy sweaters and accessories

The long sweater has raglan decreases, while the short one has set-in sleeves.
In this section you can also find a good basic pattern for gloves.

**Sizes:** S – M – L – XL
**Yarn: Rauma Finullgarn:**
**Long sweater, hat, gloves and bag**

| | |
|---|---|
| Red-lilac 470 | 14 – 15 – 16 – 17 balls |
| Green 489 | 2 –2 – 2 –2 balls |
| Dark red 499 | 1 – 1 – 1 – 1 ball |
| Red 445 | 1 – 1 – 1 – 1 ball |
| Pink 466 | 1 – 1 – 1 – 1 ball |
| Orange 461 | 1 – 1 – 1 – 1 ball |
| Dark green 476 | 1 – 1 – 1 – 1 ball |

**Short sweater, hat, scarf and mobile phone bag**

| | |
|---|---|
| Blue-lilac 474 | 9 – 10 – 11 – 12 balls |
| Green 489 | 4 – 4 – 4 – 4 balls |
| Dark red 499 | 1 – 1 – 1 – 1 ball |
| Red 445 | 1 – 1 – 1 – 1 ball |
| Pink 466 | 1 – 1 – 1 – 1 ball |
| Orange 461 | 1 – 1 – 1 – 1 ball |
| Dark green 476 | 1 – 1 – 1 – 1 ball |

**Measurements:**
Bust: 100 – 105 – 110 – 115 cm (39½ –41½ – 43½ – 45½ in)
Finished length, long sweater: 81 – 83 – 85 – 87 cm (32 – 32¾ – 33½ – 34¼ in)
Finished length, short sweater: 58 – 60 – 62 – 64 cm (23 – 23¾ – 24½ – 25¼ in)
Sleeve length: 48 – 49 – 50 – 51 cm (19 – 19⅜ – 19¾ – 20¼ in)
**Suggested needles:** Circular needle and set of 5 double-pointed needles size 5 mm
**Tension:**
**Before felting:** Approx 16 sts st st = 10 cm (4 in)
**After felting:** Approx 20 sts = 10 cm (4 in)

## Long sweater:

**Pockets:** With red-lilac, cast on 22 sts and work 25 cm (10 in) in st st in rows. Leave the stitches on a spare needle or thread them on a length of yarn. Make two pockets in this way.
**Body:** Using red-lilac and circular needle, cast on 200 – 210 – 220 – 230 sts. Work 10 rows st st. Next row: increase 10 sts evenly spaced. Continue working

in rows until work measures 36 – 36 – 38 – 38 cm (14¼ – 14¼ – 15 – 15 in). Slip 10 sts at each end of the row onto a spare needle or a length of yarn. Slip these stitches back on to the circular needle, taking one from each end alternately to form an overlapping split. Knit these 20 sts together in pairs. Change to working in rounds, casting off for the pockets on the next round as follows: the slit is at the centre front; starting from here, k 17, cast off the next 22 sts, work until 39 sts remain before the split, cast off 22 sts and k to end of round. On the next round, knit the pocket backs in place of the cast-off sts. Continue in rounds until work measures 69 – 70 – 72 – 73 cm (27¼ – 27¾ – 28½ – 29 in). Place a marker at each side, with 100 – 104 – 110 – 114 sts for the back and 100 – 106 – 110 – 116 sts for the front. Cast off 3 sts before and after each marker = 6 sts at each side. Lay the work aside and knit the sleeves.
**Sleeves:** With red-lilac, cast on 38 – 40 – 42 – 44 sts. Work in st st in rounds. Increase 1 st each side of the 2 sts at the centre underarm on every 6th round until there are 86 – 90 – 90 – 94 sts. Work straight until the sleeve measures 66 – 68 – 69 – 71 cm (26 – 26¾ – 27¼ – 28 in). Cast off 6 sts at the centre underarm.
**Raglan:** Place the sleeves on the needle between the front and back sections = 348 – 366 – 376 – 394 sts. Knit 1 round, working p2tog through the outermost stitches of each section (e.g. p last st of front tog with first st of sleeve). These 4 sts are always worked in purl. Decrease 1 st on each side of these 4 sts on every alternate round 29 – 31 – 32 – 43 times = 112 – 114 – 116 – 118 sts on needle. Slip the centre 14 – 16 – 16 – 18 sts of the front onto a thread for the neck. Continue working in rows and decreasing for the raglan and at the same time, on every alternate row, at each side of the neck opening, slip a further 3, 2, 2 sts onto

the thread, until there are 88 – 90 – 92 – 94 sts. Knit the roll collar.
**Collar:** Slip the sts from the thread onto the needle. Turn the work inside out and knit about 30 rounds st st. Cast off loosely.
**Making up:** Sew underarm edges together. Sew the pocket backs to the inside of the sweater. Turn the collar to the right side and embroider the small flower about 4 cm (1⅝ in) from the edge and 5 cm (2 in) from the centre front. Embroider the large flower on the front, about 13 cm (5¼ in) from the side and 70 – 71 – 73 – 74 cm (27½ – 28 – 28¾ – 29¼ in) from the bottom edge. Felt as described on page 8.
Embroider around the edges in blanket stitch in green.

## Hat:

With red-lilac, cast on 100 sts. Knit 40 cm (16 in) in st st in rounds. Cast off.
**Crown:** Cast on 15 sts. Work in st st in rows, increasing at each end on every alternate row 3, 2, 1, 1 sts. Then increase 1 st at each end of every 4th row twice. Continue straight until you have worked 39 rows from the cast-on edge. Decrease 1 st at each end of every 4th row twice, then on every 2nd row decrease 1, 1, 2, 3 sts at each end. Cast off.
**Making up:** Sew the crown to the hat. Fold up the brim and embroider the small flower about 4 cm (1⅝ in) from the edge. Felt as described on page 8. Embroider around the edge in blanket stitch in green.

## Bag:

With red-lilac, cast on 70 sts. K 34 cm (13½ in) in st st in rounds. Cast off. Embroider the large flower in the centre of the bag and sew the bottom edge together.

**Shoulder strap:** With red-lilac, cast on 4 sts. Work in st st in rows until the strap measures about 200 cm (79 in). Cast off. Sew the strap firmly to the sides of the bag.

Felt as described on page 8.

If desired, embroider along the top edge in blanket stitch in green.

## Short sweater:

**Body:** With blue-lilac, cast on 200 – 210 – 220 – 230 sts. Work 10 rows st st. On next row, increase 10 sts evenly spaced. Continue working in rows until work measures 29 – 29 – 31 – 31 cm (11½ – 11½ – 12¼ – 12¼ in). Slip 10 sts at each end on to a spare needle or a thread. Slip these stitches back on to the circular needle, taking one from each end alternately to form an overlapping split. Knit these 20 sts together in pairs. Change to working in rounds and knit until work measures 45 – 47 – 49 – 51 cm (17¾ – 18½ – 19½ – 20¼ in). Place a marker at each side, with 100 – 104 – 110 – 114 sts for the back and 100 – 106 – 110 – 116 sts for the front (the split should be at the centre front). Cast off 3 sts on each side of the markers = 6 sts at each side. Finish the back and front separately.

**Back:** Decrease 1 st at each end of every alternate row 3 times. Continue without shaping until work measures 77 – 80 – 83 – 86 cm (30½ – 31½ – 32¾ – 34 in). Next round cast off the middle 22 sts for the neck opening and finish each side separately. Cast off 2 sts at neck edge on every alternate row twice. Continue straight until work measures 80 – 83 – 86 – 89 cm (31½ – 32¾ – 34 – 35¼ in) and cast off.

**Front:** Knit as for back until work measures 70 – 73 – 75 – 77 cm (27¾ – 29 –29¾ – 30¾ in). Next row: cast off the middle 12 – 14 – 12 – 14 sts for the neck opening and finish each side separately. Cast off at neck edge on alternate rows 2, 2, 1, 1, 1, 1 st. Knit until work measures the same as the back and cast off.

**Sleeves:** With blue-lilac, cast on 38 – 40 – 42 – 44 sts. Work in st st in rounds. Increase 1 st each side of the 2 sts at the centre underarm on every 5th round until there are 90 – 94 – 94

– 98 sts. Work straight until the sleeve measures 66 – 68 – 69 – 71 cm (26 – 26¾ – 27¼ – 28 in). Cast off 6 sts at the centre underarm. Change to working in rows, casting off 2, 1, 1, 1 sts at each end on alternate rows. Cast off.

**Making up:**

Sew shoulder seams and set in sleeves. Pick up and knit about 80 sts around the neck edge, then cast off loosely (or you can crochet a round of dc with a 5 mm crochet hook). Embroider the large flower on the front about 47 – 49 – 51 – 53 cm (18½ – 19¼ – 20¼ – 21 in) from the bottom edge and about 10 cm (4 in) from the sleeve.

Felt as described on page 8.

Embroider around the edges in blanket stitch in green.

## Hat:

With blue-lilac, cast on 90 sts. Work 20 cm (8 in) st st in rounds. Next round: decrease by working *k7, k2tog*, rep to end of rd. Work 3 rds straight. Next round: *k6, k2tog*, rep to end. Work 3 rds straight. Continue decreasing on every 4th rd, with 1 less st between decreases each time, until 5 decreases have been worked. Then decrease on every alternate rd until 20 sts remain. Cut the yarn and thread it through the sts. Embroider the small flower about 4 cm (1¾ in) from the edge.

Felt as described on page 8.

Embroider around the edges in blanket stitch in green.

## Mobile phone bag:

With blue-lilac, cast on 32 sts. Work 18 cm (7¼ in) in st st in rounds. Cast off. Embroider the small flower about 4 cm (1¾ in) from the upper edge. Sew the bag together at the bottom.

**Handle:** With blue-lilac, cast on 4 sts. Work in st st in rows until the handle measures 20 cm (8 in) – or 200 cm (79 in) if you want a shoulder strap. Cast off. Sew the handle firmly to each side of the bag.

Felt as described on page 8.

Embroider around the upper edge in blanket stitch in green.

## Gloves:

With green yarn, cast on 34 sts. Knit 7 rds st st, increasing 4 sts evenly spaced on last rd. Continue in rounds until work measures 16 cm (6½ in). For the thumb, knit the first 6 sts of the round with a marker thread of a different colour. Slip these 6 sts back on to the lh needle. Continue in rounds until work measures 22 cm (9 in). Slip all sts on to a thread and knit the fingers as follows:

**Index finger:** Slip 6 sts from back and 6 sts from front on to 4 needles. Cast on 2 sts next to where the middle finger will be = 14 sts. K 10cm (4 in) st st in rounds. Then k2tog until 4 sts remain. Cut the yarn and pull through sts.

**Middle finger:** Slip 5 sts from back and 4 sts from front on to 4 needles. Cast on 2 sts next to where the ring finger will be and pick up and knit 2 sts from base of index finger = 13 sts. K 11cm (4⅜ in) st st in rounds and decrease as for index finger.

**Ring finger:** Slip 4 sts from back and 5 sts from front on to 4 needles. Cast on 2 sts next to where the little finger will be and pick up and knit 2 sts from base of middle finger = 13 sts. K 10cm (4 in) st st in rounds and decrease as described above.

**Little finger:** Slip the last 8 sts on to 4 needles. Pick up and knit 2 sts from ring finger = 10 sts. Knit 7 cm (2⅞ in) st st in rounds and decrease as described above.

For the second glove, work in the same way, but as a mirror image, and work the thumb over the last 6 sts of the round.

Felt as described on page 8.

## Scarf:

With green, cast on 34 sts. Work 270 cm (106 in) st st in rows. Cast off.

Felt as described on page 8.

# Fringed hat and bag

A smart, attractive hat that will keep your neck and ears warm. You could decorate the bag with a crochet rosette or a simple embroidered design (leaf through the book to find your favourite design).

**Size:** Ladies'

**Yarn: Rauma Finullgarn** (or **pt2**):
| | |
|---|---|
| Brown 411 (80) | 4 balls |
| Light brown 406 (79) | 1 ball |
| White 401 (0) | 1 ball |

**Measurements:** After felting, the bag measures approx 25 x 27 cm (10 x 10¾ in)
Shape the hat by trying it on or measuring round the head.

**Needles:** Short circular needle 40cm (16in) and set of 5 short double-pointed needles size 5 mm

**Tension before felting:**
Approx 16 sts = 10 cm (4 in)
**Tension after felting:**
Approx 20 sts = 10 cm (4 in)

## Hat:

Start with the flaps. With brown yarn, cast on 11 sts. Work in st st in rows, increasing 1 st at each side on every alternate row until there are 23 sts on needle. Work straight until the flap measures 10 cm (4 in). Knit a second flap in the same way. Put 1 flap on to the circular needle, cast on 42 sts, knit across the second flap and cast on 12 sts = 100 sts. Work in st st in rounds. When work measures about 22 cm (8¾ in) from the new cast-on edge, decrease as follows: *k8, k2tog*, rep to end of rd. Work 2 rds. Next round: *k7, k2tog*, rep to end of rd. Work 2 rds. Next round: *k6, k2tog*, rep to end of rd. Continue decreasing in this way on every 3rd rd, with 1 less st between decreases each time, until 10 sts remain. Cut the yarn and pull through sts.
**Fringes:** Each tassel consists of a light brown strand and a white strand. Cut the strands about 10 cm (4 in) long.

Knot a tassel through each stitch along the edge (all the way round, front and back and round the flaps).

## Bag:

With brown yarn, cast on 100 sts. Work about 100 rounds in st st. Cast off.
**Fringes:** Cut fringes as described for the hat. Knot a tassel in each stitch along the sides. Close up the bottom of the bag by knotting tassels through 1 st in the front and the corresponding st in the back at the same time.

Felt as described on page 8.

**Handle:** Plait a cord about 120 cm (47½ in) long using 9 strands, 3 of each colour. Tie a knot in each end. Attach the ends to each side of the bag, on the inside.

# Laced slippers

The slippers are knitted in garter stitch in rows. This makes them extra thick and warm.

**Sizes:** 4/6 yrs: ladies' – 8/10 yrs: men's

**Yarn: pt2** (or **Rauma Finullgarn**):
Suggested colours:

A: **Colour 1:** Dark grey 84 (405)
   **Colour 2:** Light grey 83 (404)
B: **Colour 1:** Red 59 (435)
   **Colour 2:** Dark grey 84 (405)
C: **Colour 1:** Pink 56
   **Colour 2:** Light brown 79
D: **Colour 1:** Blue 34
   **Colour 2:** Green 27
E: **Colour 1:** Light turquoise 30
   **Colour 2:** Dark turquoise 29

Yarn quantities:

Colour 1     1 (2) 2 (2) balls
Colour 2     2 (2) 3 (3) balls

**Suggestions for trimming:**
**For colourway B:** 8–12 red hedgehog buttons
**For colourway E:** 10–12 white 4mm beads

**Suggested needles:** Short circular needle 40cm (16in) size 6.5mm

**Tension:**
**Before felting:** Approx 10 sts garter st = 10 cm (4 in)
**After felting:** Approx 15 sts = 10 cm (4 in)

The whole project is worked in garter st in rows using double yarn.
Begin at the top. With colour 1, cast on 40 – 44 – 48 – 52 sts. Work 8 – 10 – 10 – 12 rows. Next row: k2, make 2, k2togtbl, k to about half way along the row, k2tog, k until 4 sts remain at the other end, k2tog, make 2, k2. On next row, k into first made st and drop the 2nd. Repeat the row with the holes and centre back decrease every 8th – 10th – 10th – 10th row 3 more times (= 36 – 40 – 44 – 48 sts). **NB:** Work in colour 1 up to and including 2 rows after the 3rd hole/decrease row. Change to colour 2. After the last hole/decrease row k 12 – 13 – 14 – 16 'ridges' (= 24 – 26 – 14 – 16 rows). Cast off 13 – 14 – 15 – 17 sts at each end. Work 15 – 16 – 17 – 19 'ridges' on the centre 10 – 12 – 14 – 14 sts (for the sole). Cut the yarn. Pick up and k 1 st in each of the 11 – 12 – 13 – 15 lowest 'ridges' at each side of the ankle (from the casting off up to the first ridge before the last hole). Add these sts to the needle on either side of the sole = 32 – 36 – 40 – 44 sts. Continue in garter st, casting off on 1st row for hole as described above. Continue working holes on every 8th – 10th – 10th – 10th row twice more. When you have worked 9 – 13 – 16 – 19 ridges after picking up the sts, begin decreasing for the toe as follows: Decrease 4 – 5 – 6 – 6 sts evenly spaced on 1st, 6th, 10th, 12th and 14th rows. Last row k2tog to end of row. Cut off yarn and pull through sts. Sew together on either side of the heel and on top of the toe piece as far as the first hole (the last hole you worked). With colour 1 (colour 2 for version B), knit up from the right side with double yarn 1 st between each ridge along one side of the front opening. Turn and cast off from the wrong side. Repeat along the other side.

Felt as described on page 8.

After felting, the slipper should still be a bit too big, about 2–3 cm ($\frac{3}{4}$–$1\frac{1}{4}$ in) too long and about 4–5 cm ($1\frac{5}{8}$–2 in) too wide. Put the slipper on the table and shape the sole. Tack round the sole through both layers about 1–1.5 cm ($\frac{3}{8}$–$\frac{5}{8}$ in) from the edge. Sew with backstitch from the upper side (use colour 2, double yarn).

Make laces, using two strands of each colour.

## Trimmings:

**Version A:** With colour 1 (single yarn) embroider 5 flowers in lazy daisy stitch, spread evenly just below the colour change. Embroider a cross-stitch between each flower.
**Version B:** Embroider as described for version A, but sew a hedgehog button on each cross-stitch.
**Versions C and D:** With colour 1 (double yarn) embroider a zigzag border just below the colour change.
**Version E:** With colour 2 embroider 5–6 stars around the top of the ankle. Sew a bead in the centre of each star.

# Poncho, bonnet and scarf for little girls

The poncho is made by knitting two identical rectangular pieces and sewing them together, then crocheting three rows of chains round the edge. You could also add a fringe. The bonnet is decorated with velvet ribbon and embroidery.

**Sizes:** 1 – 2 – 3 yrs
**Yarn:** pt2
**Poncho:**

| | |
|---|---|
| Green 15 | 3 – 3 – 4 balls |
| Lime 16 | 1 – 1 – 1 ball |
| Pink 54 | 1 – 1 – 1 ball |

**Scarf:**

| | |
|---|---|
| White 0 | 1 – 1 – 1 ball |

**Bonnet:**

| | |
|---|---|
| Red 53 | 1 – 1 – 1 ball |
| Light pink 55 | 1 – 1 – 1 ball |

Small amounts of leftover lime, pink and white
**Suggestions for trimming:**
**For the poncho:** One large satin flower (or several small ones)
**For the bonnet:** 100–110 cm (40–44 in) red velvet ribbon (perhaps elasticated) about 9 mm (³⁄₈ in) wide. 45–50 cm (18–20 in) white lace (about 2 cm – ⁷⁄₈ in wide)
**Suggested needles:** Circular needle, pair of needles and crochet hook size 5 mm
**Tension:**
**Before felting:** Approx 16 sts st st = 10 cm (4 in)
**After felting:** Approx 20 sts = 10 cm (4 in)
**Before felting:** Approx 18 sts garter st = 10 cm (4 in)
**After felting:** Approx 22 sts = 10 cm (4 in)

## Poncho:

With green yarn, cast on 38 – 44 – 50 sts. Work in garter st in rows until you have worked 90 – 100 – 110 'ridges' (= 180 – 200 – 220 rows). Cast off. Make two identical pieces and sew them together. See photo. With lime, crochet dc around the neck edge (crochet really tightly, perhaps 1dc in every other ridge). Crochet around the outside edge with lime, as follows:
**Round 1:** Begin at 1 corner. Work 1dc on one side of the point, 4ch and 1ss on the other side of the point, 4 ch, miss 1, *1 ss in next st, 4 ch, miss 1*, rep from * to * all the way round and finish with 1 ss in 1 st (dc).
**Round 2:** 2 ss + 4 ch + 1 ss in 1 loop, *4 ch, 1 ss in next loop, * rep from * to * as far as next corner. In the corner loop work 1 ss + 4 ch + 1 ss, *4 ch, 1 ss in next loop,* rep from * to * to end of rd.
Felt as described on page 4.
**Fringes:** Make the fringes with two strands of yarn, 1 green and 1 lime. Cut the strands about 12 cm (4¾ in) long and attach a tassel to each ch st loop.

## Rosette:

With pink yarn, crochet 7 ch, ss in first ch to form a ring.
**Round 1:** 2 ch (= first tr), work 14 more tr in ring, finish with 1ss in first tr.
**Round 2:** 1 ch (= first dc) 2 dc in next tr, *1 dc in next tr, 2 dc in next tr*, repeat from * to * = 23 dc, finish with 1 ss in first dc.
**Round 3:** 1 dc in first st, 8 ch, *1 dc in next st, 8 ch* repeat from * to * and finish with 1 ss in first dc.
Sew the satin flower in the centre of the rosette and attach the rosette to the poncho approx 4–6 cm (1⅝ –2½ in) from the bottom edge of the neck.

## Bonnet:

The bonnet is knitted in three sections: two sides and a centre section.
**Left side:** With red yarn, cast on 18 – 20 – 22 sts. Work in st st in rows, increasing 1 st at rh edge every alternate row 9 times. Continue straight until you have worked 44 – 46 – 48 rows. Decrease 1 st at rh edge on every alternate row 5 – 6 – 7 times. Cast off.

**Right side:** Work as for left side, but working all increases and decreases at lh edge.
**Centre section:** With red yarn, cast on 12 – 14 – 16 sts. Work in st st in rows, increasing 1 st at each side on every 4th row 3 times. Work until you have completed 104 – 112 – 120 rows. Cast off. Sew the bonnet together.
Felt as described on page 8.
Sew velvet ribbon along the seams. Sew the lace to the front edge. Take the rest of the velvet ribbon and mark the centre. Attach the ribbon inside, or partly over, the lace, with the centre mark at the top of the bonnet. Allow the rest of the ribbon to hang freely (for tying). Embroider the design shown in the sketch on each side of the bonnet, at an equal distance from the velvet ribbon on the top and on either side.

## Scarf:

With white yarn, cast on 23 sts. Work about 100 cm (39½ in) in st st in rows. Cast off. Crochet along the short ends as follows: 1 dc in first st, *3 ch, 1 dc in first ch (picot), miss 1, 1dc in next st*, rep from * to *.
Felt as described on page 8.

Solid line = backstitch

# Sweater, poncho, hat and bag

Simple but smart things for girls, with embroidery and decorative topstitching.

**Sizes:** 4 – 6 – 8 – 10 – 12 yrs
**Yarn:** Rauma Finullgarn (or **pt2**):
**Sweater:**
Blue-green 483 (2) 5 – 5 – 6 – 8 – 8 balls
Green 493 (17)    1 – 1 – 1 – 1 – 1 ball
**Poncho:**
Lilac 474         4 – 4 – 6 – 7 – 8 balls
Green 489         1 – 1 – 1 – 1 – 1 ball
**Hat and bag:**
Pink 465 (54)     2 – 2 – 2 – 2 – 2 balls
Lilac 442 (42)    1 – 1 – 1 – 1 – 1 ball
**Suggestions for trimming:** Transparent 4 mm beads
**Measurements:**
Chest: approx 74 – 80 – 90 – 96 – 106 cm (29½ – 31½ – 35½ – 38 – 42 in)
Overall length: approx 44 – 49 – 54 – 59 – 64 cm (17½ – 19½ – 21½ – 23½ – 25¼ in)
Sleeve length: approx 26 – 29 – 33 – 37 – 42 cm (10¼ – 11½ – 13 – 14½ – 16½ in)
Overall length, poncho: approx 33 – 38 – 45 – 51 – 56 cm (13 – 15 – 18 – 20½ – 22 in)
**Suggested needles:** Circular needle and set of 5 double-pointed needles size 5 mm. Crochet hook size 3.5 mm
**Tension:**
**Before felting:** Approx 16 sts st st = 10 cm (4 in)
**After felting:** Approx 20 sts = 10 cm (4 in)

## Sweater:

With blue-green yarn, cast on 168 – 180 – 200 – 212 – 232 sts. Place a marker at each side, with 84 – 90 – 100 – 106 – 116 sts each for the back and front. Work in rounds in st st, decreasing 1 st on each side of markers every 20th – 22nd – 24th – 26th – 28th round 5 times. Continue straight until work measures approx 44 – 49 – 53 – 58 – 62 cm (17½ – 19½ – 21 – 23 – 24½ in). Cast off 3 – 4 – 5 – 5 – 5 sts on either side of the markers = 6 – 8 – 10 – 10 – 10 at each side and finish the back and front separately.

**Back:** Decrease for armhole at each side on every alternate row 1 – 6 – 7 – 9 – 10 times. After working 45 – 50 – 57 – 62 – 69 rows from the armhole divide, cast off.

**Front:** Decrease for armhole as for back. When you have worked 12 – 15 – 18 – 21 – 24 rows from the armhole divide, part the work in the middle and finish each side separately. When you have worked 26 – 29 – 35 – 41 – 47 rows from the armhole divide, cast off 5 – 6 – 7 – 8 – 9 sts at the front for the neck. Cast off at neck edge on every alternate row 3, 2, 2, 1, 1, 1 sts. Work until front is the same length as back and cast off.

**Sleeves:** With blue-green, cast on 42 – 44 – 48 – 52 – 56 sts. Work in st st in rounds. Increase 1 st at each side of the 2 centre underarm sts on every 8th rd until there are 60 – 66 – 74 – 82 – 90 sts. Continue until you have worked about 36 – 41 – 47 – 52 – 57 cm (14¼ – 16¼ – 18½ – 20½ – 22½ in). Cast off 8 – 8 – 12 – 12 – 12 sts at centre underarm. Continue in rows and decrease for top of sleeve at each side on every alternate row 1 st 6 – 9 – 11 – 12 – 12 times and 2 sts 3 – 3 – 3 – 4 – 5 times. Cast off.

**Making up:**

Sew shoulder seams. Sew in sleeves. With doubled green yarn, topstitch around the edges with small stitches. Stitch over and under 1 st, a bare 1 cm (⅜ in) from the edge. Topstitch round the armholes in the same way.
Felt as described on page 8.
Embroider the motif in green chain stitch, about 2 cm (⅞ in) below the neck opening. Sew on beads as shown in the sketch.

## Poncho:

With lilac yarn, cast on 298 – 322 – 370 – 390 – 422 sts. Place a marker in the sts at centre front and centre back, with 148 – 160 – 184 – 194 – 210 sts in between. Then place markers half way between these, with 74 – 80 – 92 – 97 – 105 sts on each side = side markers. Work in st st in rounds, decreasing as follows: Decrease 1 st at each side of centre front and back markers every 3rd rd all the way up. At the same time, decrease 1 st each side of the side markers, leaving 2 sts in between, every 9th – 12th – 12th – 18th – 18th rd 11 – 9 – 11 – 8 – 9 times and every 3rd rd 4 – 6 – 7 – 9 – 9 times = 90 – 92 – 92 – 92 – 96 sts. Cast off.

**Pocket:** With lilac yarn, cast on 40 – 44 – 48 – 52 – 56 sts. Work 34 – 37 – 41 – 44 – 48 rows in st st. Cast off.

**Making up:**

With pink yarn used doubled, topstitch around the cast-on edge, the neck edge and the short sides of the pocket with small stitches. Stitch over and under 1 st, no more than 1 cm (⅜ in) from the edge. Topstitch down the centre front and back in the same way. Sew the pocket on firmly, using the same stitch, midway between the point at the bottom and the neck edge.

Felt as described on page 8.

Embroider the motif in pink chain stitch. Sew on beads as shown in the sketch.

## Bag:

With pink yarn, cast on 90 sts. Work 75 rounds in st st. Cast off. With double lilac yarn, topstitch with small stitches down the sides (through two layers) and along the bottom (sewing it together at the same time). Then topstitch along the top edge. Stitch over and under 1 st, a bare 1 cm (⅜ in) from the edge.

Felt as described on page 8.

Crochet a pink cord of 200 ch and ss back along it. Sew the cord firmly to each side of the bag. Embroider the motif in lilac chain stitch in the middle of one side. Sew on beads.

## Hat:

With pink yarn, cast on 86 – 90 – 90 – 96 – 100 sts. Work 36 – 38 – 40 – 42 – 44 rounds in st st. For sizes 4 yrs and 10 yrs, decrease 6 sts evenly spaced on last rd. Next round: decrease by working *k8, k2tog*, rep to end of rd. Work 3 rds without shaping. Next round: *k7, k2tog*, rep to end. Decrease in the same way on every 4th rd, with 1 less st between decreases each time, until you have worked 5 decrease rds. Then decrease every other rd until about 10 sts remain. Cut the yarn and pull through sts. With double lilac yarn, topstitch around the edge with small stitches.

Felt as described on page 8.

# Boy's sweater

A smart sweater for a boy. The scarf is taken from 'Snug sweaters and accessories' (see page 28 for pattern).

**Sizes:** 4 – 6 – 8 – 10 – 12 yrs

**Yarn:** Rauma Finullgarn (or **pt2**)

| | |
|---|---|
| Blue 443 (39) | 5 – 6 – 7 – 8 – 9 balls |
| Light blue 437 (38) | 1 – 1 – 1 – 1 – 1 ball |
| Lime 454 (16) | 2 – 2 – 2 – 2 – 2 ball |

**Measurements:**
Chest: 81 – 87 – 92 – 100 – 106 cm (32 –34½ –36½ – 39½ – 42 in)
Overall length: 40 – 45 – 50 – 55 – 60 cm (16 –18 –20 – 22 – 24 in)
Sleeve length: 42 – 47 – 51 – 55 – 59 cm (16½ –18½ – 20¼ – 21¾ – 23¼ in)

**Suggested needles:** Circular needles and set of 5 double-pointed needles sizes 4.5 and 5 mm

**Tension:**
**Before felting:** Approx 16 sts st st = 10 cm (4 in)
**After felting:** Approx 21 sts = 10 cm (4 in)

## Body:

With blue yarn and 4.5 mm needles cast on 170 – 182 – 194 – 210 – 222 sts. Work 10 rds in st st. Change to 5 mm needles and continue in rds until you have worked 77 – 87 – 103 – 112 – 127 rds. Divide the work at the sides, with 85 – 91 – 97 – 105 – 111 sts for back and front, and complete each side separately.

**Back:**
Work 59 – 63 – 67 – 73 – 77 rows st st. Cast off.

**Front:**
Work as for back until 38 – 44 – 46 – 51 – 53 rows have been completed. Cast off 11 – 13 – 15 – 17 – 19 sts at centre and complete each side separately. Decrease at neck edge on every alternate row 3, 2, 2, 1, 1 sts. Work until front is same length as back and cast off.

## Sleeves:

With blue yarn and 4.5 mm needles, cast on 42 – 44 – 48 – 52 – 56 sts. Work 10 rds st st. Change to 5 mm needles and continue in rds, increasing 2 sts at centre underarm on every 5th round until you have 78 – 84 – 88 – 94 – 98 sts. Work straight until 97 – 110 – 119 – 131 – 143 rds have been completed. Cast off loosely.

## Pocket:

With blue yarn and 5 mm needles, cast on 45 – 49 – 53 – 57 – 61 sts. Work 20 – 22 – 24 – 26 – 28 rows st st. Then decrease 1 st at each side on every alternate row 8 – 9 – 10 – 11 – 12 times. Cast off. Sew shoulder seams and set in sleeves.
Felt sweater and pocket as described on page 8.

With lime yarn, topstitch along the sloping edges of the pocket. Position the pocket at the centre front, about 4 cm (1⅝ in) from the cast-on edge. Sew firmly in place with small topstitches in lime. Topstitch around the bottom edge of the body and cuffs and around the neck opening (about 7 mm (¼ in) from the edge).

## Mittens:

With lime yarn, cast on 34 sts. Knit 7 rds st st, increasing 4 sts evenly spaced on last rd. Continue in rounds until work measures 16 cm (6½ in). For the thumb, knit the first 6 sts of the round with a marker thread of a different colour. Slip these 6 sts back on to the lh needle. Continue in rounds until the mitten measures 28 cm (11 in). Place a marker at each side, at the beginning of the round and after 19 sts. Cast off 1 st on each side of the markers on every alternate round until 6 sts remain. Cut the yarn and pull it through the sts.
**Thumb:** Remove the marker thread and slip the stitches on to 4 needles. Pick up and knit 1 st at each side (= 14 sts). Work 8 cm st st. Then k2tog until 4 sts remain. Cut off yarn and pull it through the stitches.
For the second mitten, work the thumb over the last 6 stitches of the round.
Felt as described on page 8.

# Beautiful bag, mittens and hat

A smart, stylish hat, with a sewn-in hatband so it sits properly. The mittens have splendid shaggy fringes. The windowpane check pattern on the bag is achieved by knitting stripes in rounds and then embroidering the vertical stripes in stem stitch.

**Size:** Ladies'

**Yarn: Rauma Finullgarn**

| | |
|---|---|
| Light grey 403 | 2–3 balls |
| Grey 405 | 1 ball |
| Light lilac 471 | 1 ball |
| Lilac 4088 | 1 ball |
| Dark lilac 474 | 2 balls |

**Suggestions for trimming:** Light lilac (or grey) sequins. You will also need a 20 cm (8 in) zip for the bag, and a 60–65 cm (24–26 in) hatband for the hat.

**Measurements:** After felting, the bag measures approx 32 x 20 cm (12¾ x 8 in)

Shape the hat by trying it on or measuring round the head.

**Suggested needles:** Short circular needle 40cm (16in) size 5 mm

**Tension:**

**Before felting:** Approx 16 sts = 10 cm (4 in)

**After felting:** Approx 20 sts = 10 cm (4 in)

## Mittens:

With light grey yarn, cast on 36 sts. Work 7cm (2⅞ in) st st in rounds, increasing 4 sts evenly over last rd. Continue in st st until work measures 16 cm (6⅜ in). For the thumb, knit the first 7 sts of the round with a marker thread of a different colour. Slip these 7 sts back on to the lh needle. Continue straight until work measures about 30 cm (12 in). Then place a marker at each side, at the start of the round and after 20 sts. Decrease 1 st on each side of the markers on every alternate rd 6 times (= 16 sts). Graft together.

**Thumb:** Remove the marker thread and slip the stitches on to 4 needles. Pick up and knit 1 st at each side (= 16 sts). Work 8 cm st st. Then k2tog until 4 sts remain. Cut off yarn and thread it through the stitches.

For the second mitten, work the thumb over the last 7 stitches of the round.

**Fringes:** Each tassel consists of 4 strands, one of each colour. Use all 5 colours, putting them together in slightly different combinations. Cut them about 12cm (5 in) long and attach them along the cast-on edge in every other stitch.

## Hat:

With lilac yarn, cast on 180 sts. Work 4 rds in st st. Round 5: decrease by working *k7, k2tog*, rep to end. Work 4 rds. Next round: decrease by working *k6, k2tog* rep to end. Work 4 rds. Next round: *k5, k2tog* rep to end. Work 4 rds. Next round: *k4, k2tog* rep to end = 100 sts. Work 28 rds. Next round: decrease by working *k8, k2tog* rep to end. Work 2 rds. Next round: *k7, k2tog* rep to end. Continue decreasing in the same way on every 3rd round, with 1 stitch less between decreases each time until 10 sts remain. Cut the yarn and pull through sts.

Mark the round after the last decrease for the brim with a tacking thread. Measure round your head and add 3cm (1⅜ in) to give you the length of the hatband. Sew the ends of the hatband together with a 1.5cm (⅝ in) seam. Press the seam open. Pin the band to the inside of the hat, just above the tacking thread. Tack it firmly in place, then sew along the top and bottom edges with small stitches. Sew sequins along the edge of the brim, about 0.5 cm (¼ in) from the cast-on edge and about the same distance apart.

## Bag:

With light grey yarn, cast on 128 sts. Work 5 rds st st. Then work *1 rd grey, 1 rd light grey, 1 rd lilac, 1 rd light grey, 1 rd dark lilac, 9 rds light grey*. Repeat from * to * three more times = 5 stripes. Work 5 rds in light grey. Cast off.

**Vertical stripes:** (Begin anywhere on the work.) Embroider the stripes in stem stitch, with 1 st between each stripe. Embroider one stripe in grey, one lilac and one dark lilac. Miss 8 sts and repeat the stripes. Continue in the same way all the way round. Sew together along the bottom (making sure the stripes match up).

Felt as described on page 8.

**Making up:** Sew the zip in the middle of the top of the bag. With light grey yarn, make two x 25cm (10 in) cords of double yarn. Tie knots at each end. Fasten them to each side of the bag. Tie a bow inside the bag, pulling the edges in to form the shape shown in the photo.

**Handles:** Plait two x 17 cm (7 in) long handles using 5 strands, one of each colour. Make knots at each end. Attach the handles to each side, at the ends of the zip.

# Fringed slippers

These cute slippers are knitted in rows in garter stitch and sewn together.

**Size:** Ladies'

**Yarn: pt2** (or **Rauma Finullgarn**)

| | |
|---|---|
| Blue 7051 | 3 balls |
| Light grey 7003 | 1 ball |
| Petrol 7025 | 1 ball or leftovers (may be joined) |
| Light blue 7032 | 1 ball or leftovers (may be joined) |

**Measurements:** Shape the slippers to fit the feet.

**Suggested needles:** Short circular needle 40cm (16in) size 6mm

**Tension:**

**Before felting:** Approx 13 sts garter st = 10cm (4in)

**After felting:** Approx 16 sts = 10cm (4in)

With blue yarn, cast on 48 sts. Work 13 'ridges' (= 26 rows). Cast off 17 sts at each side. Work 19 ridges on the central 14 sts (= sole). Cut the yarn. Pick up 1 st in each of the bottom ridges of the ankle. Put these sts on the needle on each side of the sole (= 40 sts). Work 14 ridges. Decrease for toe: decrease 6 sts evenly spaced across 1st, 6th, 10th, 12th and 14th rows. Work k2tog across the final row. Cut the yarn and pull through the sts.

Sew together at each side of the heel. Begin at the 5th ridge from where you began picking up for the ankle and sew together along the top of the foot.

**Fringes:** Cut strands 24cm (9½in) long, mainly of light grey yarn, but also a few strands of the other colours. Use three strands for each tassel and attach them around the opening of the slipper, in the second ridge from the edge, one tassel in each stitch.

# Beaded basket

This basket is very quick and easy to knit. It can be given a matching lining, stiffened with iron-on interfacing and used as a cache-pot.

**Yarn: Røros Lamullgarn**
Light grey L12        1 ball
**Suggestions for trimming:**
Large faceted beads and silver tube beads or small beads. Beading thread. Possibly a little cardboard and corrugated paper to give the basket shape. If you want to line the basket, you will need 20 cm (8 in) fabric in a matching colour and iron-on interfacing.
**Measurements:** Approx 14 cm (5½ in) diameter
**Suggested needles:** Short circular needle 40 cm (16 in) and 4 short double-pointed needles size 4 mm
**Tension:**
**Before felting:** Approx 18 sts st st = 10 cm (4 in)
**After felting:** Approx 22 sts = 10 cm (4 in)

Cast on 80 sts. Work 45 rds st st. Knit the hole pattern by working *k2tog, yfd*, rep to end of rd. Work 2 more rds st st. Next round: decrease by working *k6, k2tog*, rep to end. Work 2 rds. Next round, decrease by working *k5, k2tog* to end of round. Continue decreasing on every 3rd rd, with 1 less st between decreases each time, until 10 sts remain. Cut off yarn and pull through sts.
Felt as described on page 8.
Cut a circle of card/cardboard the size of the basket (measure the diameter to be on the safe side). Place this in the bottom. Measure the circumference of the basket, and cut corrugated card to fit. Tape the ends together and place it inside the basket. Leave it there until the basket is completely dry.
Fold about 2.5 cm (1 in) over to the outside. Attach beads about 1 cm (⅜ in) apart. You could substitute 4–5 small beads for the tube beads.
The basket could well be lined. Use the pieces you cut out of cardboard as a pattern, cutting off the top 3 cm (1¼ in). Add 1 cm (⅜ in) along all sides. Cut out two pieces for the bottom and two for the sides. Iron interfacing on one bottom and one side piece. Sew the short edges of the side piece together and sew to the bottom. With right sides together, sew the lining to the basket at the top, but leave a small opening for turning the work right side out. Sew up the opening by hand.

45

# Angel

Beads, satin roses and feathers make this the cutest angel...

**Yarn: Rauma Finullgarn** (or **pt2**)
White 401 (0)      1 ball

**Suggestions for trimming:**
White doll's hair, white feathers, 12 small satin roses, small white, transparent, pink and green beads, 14 slightly bigger beads (4–5 mm), white beading thread. For the head, you can use a ready-painted 3 cm (1¼ in) wooden ball, or you can paint the face yourself on a plain wooden ball. To attach the head, you will need a piece of cane or dowelling that fits the hole in the ball. In addition, you will need glue for assembling the angel, a little rice and some cotton wool.

**Measurements:** After felting, including the head, the angel measures about 17 cm (6¾ in)

**Suggested needles:** Set of 5 double-pointed needles size 5 mm

**Tension:**
**Before felting:** Approx 16 sts st st = 10 cm (4 in)
**After felting:** Approx 20 sts = 10 cm (4 in)

Cast on 50 sts. Work in st st in rounds, decreasing 5 sts evenly spaced on every 6th rd 7 times = 15 sts remaining. Continue straight until you have worked 45 rds. Cast off. Pick up 50 sts along bottom edge. Work 1 rd purl and 1 rd plain. Next round, decrease by working *k3, k2tog*, rep to end of round. Work 2 rds st st. Next round:

decrease by working *k2, k2tog*, rep to end of round. Work 2 rds st st. Next round: *k1, k2tog*, rep to end of round. Next rd, k2tog to end of round = 10 sts. Cut the yarn and pull through stitches.
**Wings:** Cast on 30 sts. Work about 15 cm (6in) in st st in rows. Cast off.

Felt as described on page 8.

**Making up:** Begin with the wings. Cut them out using the pattern below. Sew stem stitch and backstitch as shown in the sketch. Stick feathers in through the stitches on the back. You could sew a few extra stitches to ensure the feathers are firmly fixed. Pour a little rice into the bottom of the angel to make it firm. Fill it up with cotton wool (be sparing with the cotton wool). Cut the cane or dowel

a little shorter than the angel's body. Glue the head firmly to one end and leave to dry. Push the cane down into the body. Knot some woollen yarn around the neck to make a little collar and hold the head in place. Pull the head up a bit. Spread glue on the inside of the collar, push the head down, and leave to dry. Make a cord of double yarn about 25 cm (10 in) long. Tie a knot in each end and two knots in the middle. This makes the angel's arms. Sew the end knots firmly behind the neck. Sew the wings to the centre back with a vertical seam. Glue doll's hair to the angel's head. Make a string of beads 16 cm (6⅜ in) long, using small beads of different colours, with some big beads in between and three roses. Hang the string of beads over the angel's 'hands' (the knots in the middle).

Pattern for wings

# Decorative heart

This heart looks great on the Christmas tree or in the window. You could decorate it with beads, satin roses or with decorative stitching.

**Yarn: Rauma Finullgarn** (or **pt2**)
Red 418 (88)        1 ball
**Trimmings:** Here we have used a Christmas decoration cut in pieces of a suitable length and fixed to the heart, but you could also use beads, e.g.

6 mm pearlised faceted beads with small transparent beads in between. The loop for hanging is made of beading thread.
For 5 hearts: cast on 70 sts. Work 90 rows st st. Cast off.

Felt as described on page 8.
Cut out hearts using the pattern.

Pattern for heart

# Heart basket

This basket is quick and easy to knit and creates a lovely Christmas mood.

**Yarn: Rauma Finullgarn** (or **pt2**)
Red 418 (88)        1 ball
White 401 (10)      1 ball
**Measurements:** Approx 18 cm (7¼ in) diameter
**Suggested needles:** Short circular needle 40cm (16in) and set of 5 double-pointed needles size 5 mm

**Tension:**
**Before felting:** Approx 16 sts st st = 10 cm (4 in)
**After felting:** Approx 20 sts = 10 cm (4 in)

With red yarn, cast on 80 sts. Work 50 rounds st st. Then knit the row of holes by repeating *k2tog, yfd*. Work 2 rds st st. Next round: decrease by working *k6, k2tog*, rep to end. Work 2 rds st st. Next round: decrease by working *k5, k2tog*, rep to end. Continue decreasing on every 3rd rd, with 1 less st between decreases each time until 10 sts remain. Cut the yarn and pull through sts.
With white yarn, cast on 30 sts. Work 40 rows st st. Cast off.
Felt as described on page 8.

Shape the basket using cardboard as described for the white basket with red roses on page 50.
Cut out the heart using the pattern and sew it on with small stitches in red yarn. Topstitch in white with small stitches around the top, about 7 mm (¼ in) from the edge.
You may like to line the basket. Follow the instructions for the white basket with roses, but only cut off a bare 1 cm (about ⅜ in) from the top edge of the cardboard shape.

# Christmas basket

Knit a simple but attractive basket for Christmas biscuits or cakes.

**Yarn: Røros Lamullgarn**
White L11          1 ball

**Suggestions for trimming:**
11 large satin roses (or more smaller ones). If you wish to line the basket, you will need 20 cm (8 in) fabric in a matching colour and iron-on interfacing.

**Measurements:** Approx 14 cm (5⅝ in) diameter

**Suggested needles:** Short circular needle 40 cm (16 in) and set of 5 double-pointed needles size 4 mm

**Tension:**
**Before felting:** Approx 18 sts st st = 10 cm (4 in)
**After felting:** Approx 22 sts = 10 cm (4 in)

Cast on 80 sts. Work 45 rounds st st. Then knit the row of holes by repeating *k2tog, yfd*. Work 2 rds st st. Next round: decrease by working *k6, k2tog*, rep to end. Work 2 rds st st. Next round: decrease by working *k5, k2tog*, rep to end. Continue decreasing on every 3rd rd, with 1 less st between decreases each time until 10 sts remain. Cut the yarn and pull through sts.

Felt as described on page 8.

Cut a circle of card/cardboard the size of the basket (measure the diameter to be on the safe side). Place this in the bottom. Measure the circumference of the basket, and cut corrugated card to fit. Tape the ends together and place it inside the basket. Leave it there until the basket is completely dry.

Fold about 2.5 cm (1 in) over to the outside. Sew the roses evenly spaced around the top on the right side.

The basket can be lined. Use the pieces you cut out of cardboard as a pattern, cutting off the top 3 cm (1¼ in). Add 1 cm (⅜ in) along all sides. Cut out two pieces for the bottom and two for the sides. Iron interfacing on one bottom and one side piece. Sew the short edges of the side piece together and sew to the bottom. With right sides together, sew the lining to the basket at the top, but leave a small opening for turning the work right side out. Sew up the opening by hand.

# Red mat

A mat with crocheted edges knitted from leftover yarn used double.

**Yarn: Rauma Finullgarn** (or **pt2**)
Red 435 (59)          2 balls
Light grey 403 (82)    1 ball

**Measurements:** Approx 25 x 25 cm (10 x 10 in) diameter

**Suggested needles:** Short circular needle 40 cm (16 in) size 6.5 mm and crochet hook size 5 mm

**Tension:**
**Before felting:** Approx 11 sts garter st = 10 cm (4 in)
**After felting:** Approx 15 sts = 10 cm (4 in)

With red yarn used double, cast on 35 sts. Work in garter st in rows until you have completed 35 ridges. Cast off. Crochet around the edges in grey as follows: begin at the cast-on edge with 1 dc in 2nd st, 3 ch, 1 dc in first ch (= picot), miss 1 st, 1 dc in next st, *1 picot, miss 1, 1 dc in next st*, rep from * to * as far as the corner. 1 picot, 1 dc between first and 2nd ridges, 1 picot, 1 dc between 3rd and 4th ridges, 1 picot, 1 dc between 5th and 6th ridges and so on to next corner, 1 picot and 1 dc in 2nd st along the cast-off edge, continue as described above. Finish with a loop of 12 ch and 1 ss in first dc.

# Rococo bag

The design is embroidered in chain stitch and then outlined in stem stitch before felting. Finally the bag is decorated with velvet ribbon tied at the sides.

**Yarn: pt2**

| | |
|---|---|
| Dark green 25 | 2 balls |
| Pink 50 | 1 ball |

**Suggestions for trimming:**
150 cm (60 in) pink velvet ribbon approx 1.5 cm (⅝ in) wide, 4 large silvery beads with large holes and 11 x 4 mm pink beads

**Measurements:** After felting, the bag measures approx 28 x 28 cm (11 x 11 in)

**Suggested needles:** Short circular needle 40 cm (16 in) size 5 mm

**Tension:**
**Before felting:** Approx 16 sts st st = 10 cm (4 in)
**After felting:** Approx 20 sts = 10 cm (4 in)

With dark green yarn, cast on 120 sts. Work 100 rounds in st st. Cast off. Embroider the design in chain stitch and stem stitch about 14 rds from the cast-on edge.

**Handles:** Cast on 50 sts. Work 10 rows in st st. Cast off. Sew the cast-on and cast-off edges together.

Felt as described on page 8.

Sew on the handles about 8 cm (3¼ in) from the sides. Sew the bag together along the bottom. Sew the velvet ribbon to the back and front, about 2.5 cm (1 in) from the top edge (leave the last 2–3 cm (⅞–1¼ in) hanging loose). Thread a large bead on each of the 4 ends and fasten it with a pink bead at the end. Sew pink beads on the front of the bag as shown in the chart. Tie the ribbon in bows at each side.

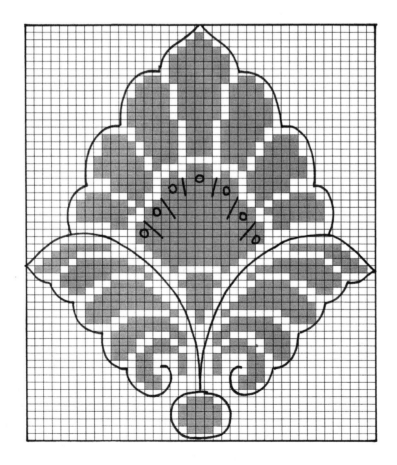

# Embroidered cushion

You could knit several matching cushions and decorate them with crochet rosettes and different designs (leaf through the book and choose your favourite designs).

**Yarn: Rauma Finullgarn**

| | |
|---|---|
| Green 489 | 2 balls |
| Dark green 486 | 1 ball |
| Lime 454 | 1 ball |
| Lilac 474 | 1 ball |
| White 401 | 1 ball |

**Measurements:** After felting, the cushion measures approx 40 x 40 cm (16 x 16 in)

**Suggested needles:** Circular needle size 5 mm

**Tension:**
**Before felting:** Approx 16 sts st st = 10 cm (4 in)
**After felting:** Approx 20 sts = 10 cm (4 in)

With green yarn, cast on 160 sts. Work 55 cm (22 in) st st in rounds. Cast off. Sew together along one side. Leave the other side (the bottom) open.

Felt as described on page 8.

Embroider the design as shown in the sketch. Insert cushion pad and sew the bottom edges together.

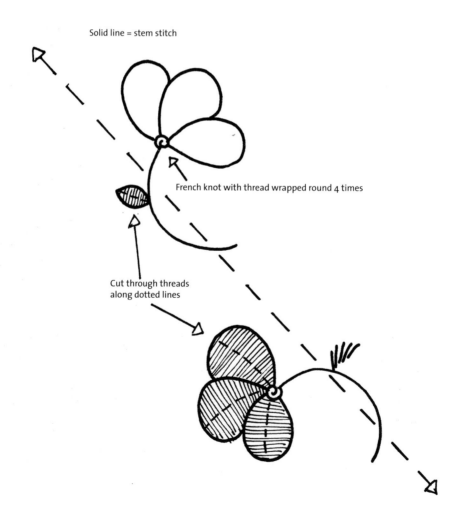

Solid line = stem stitch

French knot with thread wrapped round 4 times

Cut through threads along dotted lines

# Crocheted rug

You can make the rug whatever size you want. It is very easy to add (or subtract) as many repeats as you like (16 sts x 8 rows).

**Yarn: Røros Lamullgarn**
White L11          11 balls

**Measurements:** After felting, the rug measures approx 110 x 150 cm (44 x 60 in)

**Suggested needles:** Crochet hook size 4–5 mm

**Before felting:** one repeat measures approx 8 x 9.5 cm (3¼ x 3¾ in)
**After felting:** one repeat measures approx 6.5 x 8 cm (2¾ x 3¼ in)
One repeat = 16 sts and 8 rows

Make 263 ch. Then follow the chart. Repeat rows 1–8 18 times and finish with rows 9 and 10.

**Crochet around the edges as follows:**
**Round 1:** Begin in the corner loop of one short side and work 4 ch (= 1 dbl tr) + 2 dbl tr. Continue with 1 dbl tr in/round every st. In the next corner loop work 5 dbl tr. Along the long side, work alternately 2 and 3 dbl tr round each tr. Work 5 dbl tr in the corner loop and continue along the second short side and the second long side as described above. Finish with 2 dbl tr in the last corner loop.
**Round 2:** 1 dc in first dbl tr, 4 ch, *miss 3 dbl tr, 1 dc in next dbl tr, 4 ch*. Repeat from * to * and finish with 1 ss in first dc.
**Round 3:** 2 ss + 1 dc in 1st ch st loop, 6 tr in next ch st loop, *1 dc in next ch st loop, 6 tr in next ch st loop*. Repeat from * to * and finish with 1 ss in first dc.

Felt as described on page 8, but at 30°C. Use a very gentle wash programme.

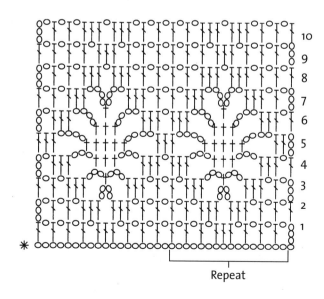

10
9
8
7
6
5
4
3
2
1

Repeat

O = ch
† = dc
Ⲧ = tr

# Furry hat and mittens

Knit these lovely mittens and hat with sewn-on crochet motifs.

**Size:** Ladies'
**Yarn:** pt2
Light brown 67     3 balls
White 0          1 ball
**Measurements:** Shape the mittens to fit the hands. Shape the hat by trying on or measuring round your head.
**Suggested needles:** Short circular needle 40cm (16in) and set of 5 double-pointed needles size 5mm. Crochet hook size 3mm
**Tension:**
**Before felting:** Approx 16 sts st st = 10cm (4in)
**After felting:** Approx 20 sts = 10cm (4in)

## Hat:

With light brown yarn, cast on 120 sts and work in rounds as follows: Round 1: *k29, p1*, rep to end. Round 2: knit. Repeat these two rounds all the way up (the purl stitch makes the marker for attaching the fringes). Continue until work measures 23cm (9¼in). Next round: Decrease 1 st on each side of the marker sts by working k2tbl before the marker st and k2tog after it. Decrease in this way on every 4th rd twice more. Then decrease on every 3rd rd twice and then every other rd until 24 sts remain. Then work k2, k2tog on every alternate rd twice. Cut the yarn and thread it through the sts.

**Fringes:** Cut white yarn into 10cm (4in) lengths. Use three strands for each tassel. Attach the tassels through two threads (sts), the marker st and the st above it, all the way up along the four lines of markers. Attach fringes around the bottom edge as well, 1 tassel in each st, 1 row above the cast-on edge. Trim the fringes to about 2.5cm (1in).

## Mittens:

With light brown, cast on 62 sts. Work in st st in rounds, decreasing 4 sts evenly spaced on every 8th rd 4 times = 46 sts. Continue straight until work measures 17cm (6¾in). Next round: for the thumb gusset, increase 1 st on each side of the first stitch of the round. Work 4 rds. Next round: increase 1 st on each side of the same stitch as in the previous increase round. Increase in the same way on every 5th rd, so there will always be 2 more sts between the increased sts, until there are 9 sts in the gusset (54 sts on needle). Continue until work measures 26cm (10¼in). Slip the 9 sts of the gusset on to a thread. Cast on 9 sts over these and work 11cm (4½in) in rounds. Next round: decrease 6 sts evenly spaced. Work 6 rds without shaping. Decrease 6 sts evenly spaced. Work 5 rds without shaping. Continue decreasing 6 sts over the round, with 1 rd less between decreases each time, until 6 sts remain. Cut the yarn and pull through sts.

**Thumb:** Slip the sts from the thread on to a needle. Pick up and knit the 9 cast-on sts + 1 st at each side = 20 sts. Work 7cm (2¾in) st st in rounds. Next round: decrease 4 sts evenly spaced. Work 2 rds without shaping. Decrease 4 sts evenly spaced on every 3rd rd twice more = 8 sts. Cut the yarn and thread it through the sts.

**Fringes:** Cut white yarn into 10cm (4in) lengths. Use three strands for each tassel. Attach the tassels along the edge of the mittens, with one tassel in each stitch, 1cm (⅜in) from the cast-on edge. Trim the fringes to about 2.5cm (1in). Felt as described on page 4.

For the motifs, crochet 6 cords of 70ch (about 28cm – 11in). Pin the cords to the articles as shown in the sketch, or in any design you like. Sew them on with backstitch (one stitch in each chain).

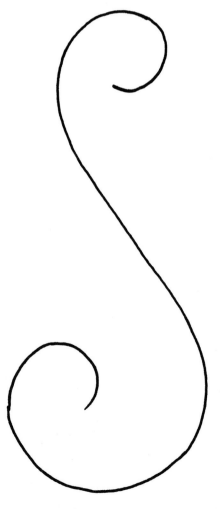

# Chic sweaters with accessories

Elegant garments with a simple bead trim.

**Sizes:** XXS – XS – S – M – L
**Yarn: pt2** (or **Rauma Finullgarn**)
White 0 (401) or grey 82 (403)
**Sweater:** 6 – 7 – 7 – 8 – 9 balls
**Hat:** 1 ball
**Scarf:** 1 ball
**Bag:** 1 ball
**Suggestions for trimming:**
Dark grey beads or gemstones for the grey sweater
Pale pink beads or gemstones for the white sweater
**Measurements:**
Bust: 84 – 90 – 94 – 98 – 104 cm (33 – 35½ – 37 – 38½ – 41 in)
Overall length: 58 – 60 – 62 – 64 – 66 cm (23 – 23¾ – 24½ – 25¼ – 26 in)
Sleeve length: 45 – 46 – 47 – 48 – 49 cm (17¾ – 18¼ – 18⅝ – 19 – 19⅜ in)
**Suggested needles:** Circular needle and set of 5 double-pointed needles size 5 mm
**Tension:**
**Before felting:** Approx 16 sts st st = 10 cm (4 in)
**After felting:** Approx 20 sts = 10 cm (4 in)

## Sweater:

**Back:**
Cast on 84 – 90 – 94 – 98 – 104 sts. Work in st st in rows, decreasing 1 st at each side, one stitch from the edge, on every 14th row 5 times. Continue until work measures 33 – 33 – 35 – 35 – 36 cm (13 – 13 – 13⅞ – 13⅞ – 14¼ in). Then increase 1 st at each side on every 8th row 5 times. Continue until work measures 51 – 53 – 55 – 57 – 59 cm (20¼ – 21 – 21¾ – 22½ – 23¼ in). Cast off 6 – 6 – 6 – 8 – 8 sts at each side. Continue decreasing 1 st at each side for the armhole on every alternate row 5 times. Continue until work measures 76 – 79 – 82 – 84 – 87 cm (30 – 31¼ – 32⅜ – 33¼ – 34⅜ in). Cast off the centre 22 – 22 – 24 – 24 – 24 sts for the neck and complete each side separately. Decrease at neck edge on next and following alternate rows 2 sts then 1 st. Knit until work measures 80 – 83 – 86 – 88 – 91 cm (31½ – 32¾ – 34 – 34¾ – 35½ in). Cast off.

**Front:** Work as for back until work measures 54 – 55 – 58 – 59 – 62 cm (21⅜ – 21¾ – 23 – 23⅜ – 24½ in). Divide the work at centre front and complete each side separately. When work measures 69 – 72 – 75 – 77 – 80 cm (27¼ – 28½ – 29½ – 30½ – 31⅝ in), cast off 6 – 6 – 7 – 7 – 7 sts for the neck opening. Continue decreasing 1 st at neck edge on every alternate row 14 – 14 – 16 – 16 – 17 times and 2 sts 2 – 2 – 1 – 1 – 1 time(s). Cast off.

**Sleeves:**
Cast on 46 – 48 – 50 – 52 – 54 sts. Work 14 cm (5½ in) st st in rows. **Change to working in rounds** and continue until work measures 30 – 31 – 33 – 35 – 36 cm (12 – 12⅜ – 13 – 13⅞ – 14¼ in). Then increase 2 sts at underarm every 4th round until there are 64 – 66 – 68 – 70 – 72 sts. Continue until work measures 62 – 63 – 65 – 67 – 68 cm (24½ – 24⅞ – 25¾ – 26½ – 26⅞ in). Cast off 12 sts at centre underarm. Cast off 1 st at each side on every alternate row 14 – 14 – 16 – 16 – 17 times and 2 sts 2 – 2 – 1 – 1 – 1 time(s). Cast off.

**Making up:**
Sew shoulder seams. Sew side seams, leaving 22 cm (8¾ in) open at the bottom for the splits. Sew in the sleeves.
Felt as described on page 8.
Sew beads (gemstones) along the edges of the neck slit. Sew them in 2 rows, the first about 1 cm (⅜ in) from the edge and the second 2 cm (⅞ in) from the edge, leaving about 1 cm (⅜ in) between the beads in each row. Sew 5 rows of beads around the bottoms of the sleeves as well, but with the first row right at the edge.

## Hat:

Cast on 90 sts. Join into a ring. Work 22 cm (8¾ in) st st in rounds. Next round decrease by working *k7, k2tog*, rep to end. Work 3 rds st st. Next round: decrease by working *k6, k2tog* rep to end. Work 3 rds st st. Continue decreasing on every 4th rd, with 1 less stitch between decreases each time, 5 times in all. Then decrease on every alternate rd until 20 sts remain. Cut the yarn and pull through sts.
Felt as described on page 8.
Sew beads about 1 cm (⅜ in) from the edge of the hat and sew another row of beads about 5 cm (2 in) from the top of the hat.

## Scarf:

Cast on 35 sts. Work 270 cm (106 in) st st in rows. Cast off.
Felt as described on page 8.
Sew 3 rows of beads at each end, with the first row right at the edge.

## Bag:

Cast on 70 sts. Join into a ring. Work 34 cm (13½ in) st st in rounds. Cast off. Sew together along the bottom.
**Strap:** Crochet a cord about 180 cm (70 in) in length using triple yarn. Attach it to either side of the bag.
Felt as described on page 8.
Sew 2 rows of beads along the top, with about 1 cm (⅜ in) between them.

# Black evening bag

The thin silver yarn knitted in with the wool makes the bag sparkle. The fur trim adds an exclusive touch.

**Yarn: Rauma Finullgarn** (or **pt2**)
Black 436 (4)          2 balls
1 spool thin silver thread (sewing thread)

**Suggestions for trimming:** For this bag, we used 1 m (39 in) thick black ribbon with silver glitter and a fur edge. As an alternative, you could use 1 m (39 in) ribbon with faux fur and 60 cm (24 in) thick/stiff black ribbon about 1.5 cm (⅝ in) wide.
1 large silver bead (8 mm)

**Measurements:** After felting, the bag measures approx 28 x 18 cm (11 x 7¼ in)

**Suggested needles:** Short circular needle 40 cm (16 in) size 5 mm. Crochet hook size 5 mm

**Tension:**
**Before felting:** Approx 13–14 sts garter st = 10 cm (4 in)
**After felting:** Approx 17 sts = 10 cm (4 in)

Using silver thread and wool together, cast on 60 sts. Work 50 'ridges' garter st in rows. Cast off loosely. Fold in two and sew down sides, starting from 9th stitch (= opening at top of each side). Pick up one stitch at the edge of each ridge = 25 sts. Work 4 ridges garter st in rows. Cast off loosely. Do the same along the other side.

**Handle:** Crochet 40 ch. Work 1 tr in 5th ch from hook and each of the following ch. Make two handles the same and attach them to the top of each side.

Felt as described on page 8.

## Rosette:

Crochet the rosette as follows: using wool only, make 7 ch and join in a ring with 1 ss in first ch.
**Round 1:** 2 ch (= 1st tr), 14 more tr in ring, finish with 1 ss in first tr.
**Round 2:** 2 ch (= 1st tr), 2 tr in each tr = 30 tr, finish with 1 ss in first tr.
**Round 3:** 2 ch (= 1st tr), 2tr in next tr, *1 tr in next tr, 2 tr in next tr*, rep from * to * = 45 tr, finish with 1 ss in 1st tr.
Measure the circumference of the rosette and add 5 cm (2 in). Cut this length of fur ribbon and sew it round the edge of the rosette, on the back. Attach a bead in the middle. Sew the rosette firmly in the centre of the bag. Cut 2 x 32 cm (12¾ in) lengths of fur ribbon. Sew the ribbon to the garter st border along the top. To give the bag a firm edge, it should cover the outside and the inside (start and end on the inside and overlap the ends of the ribbon by about 1 cm – ⅜ in).

# Fringed poncho

This elegant poncho is knitted in garter stitch in rows. The collar is worked in rows in rib. The loose sleeves are worked in stocking stitch in rounds, increasing and decreasing for the elbow. The cuffs are edged with the same pattern as the collar.

**Size:** Ladies'
**Yarn:** pt2 (or **Rauma Finullgarn**)
White 0 (401)        14 balls
**Measurements:**
Width: 110 cm (43½ in)
Overall length: 59 cm (23¼ in)
Sleeve length: 58 cm (23 in)
**Suggested needles:** Circular needle and set of 5 double-pointed needles size 5 mm
**Tension:**
**Before felting:** Approx 14 sts garter st = 10 cm (4 in)
**After felting:** Approx 16 sts = 10 cm (4 in)

## Poncho:

Start with the fringes. Cast on 5 sts. Work 1 row plain. Do not turn the work, push the sts back to the other end of the needle and knit them from the same side. Repeat until fringe measures 10 cm (4 in). Do not cast off, cut the yarn and slip the 5 sts on to the circular needle. Repeat until you have 29 fringes on the circular needle. Work 1 row plain across all the fringes, casting on 2 sts between each fringe = 201 sts. Work 38 cm (15 in) garter st in rows. Cast off the centre 17

sts for the neck. Complete each side separately. Cast off at neck edge on every alternate row 4, 2, 1, 1, 1, 1 sts. Work 4 more rows. Continue with the back. Increase at neck edge on every alternate row 1, 2, 3 sts. (Work the other side to match.) Cast on 25 sts for back of neck (= 201 sts again) and continue knitting garter st in rows until back measures the same as front. Make a fringe as described above. Cast off 2 sts. Repeat until you have made 29 fringes.

## Collar:

Beginning at centre front, on wrong side of work, pick up and knit 105 sts around neck edge. Then beginning on right side of collar (the side that will be outside when the collar is turned down), work 7 cm (2¾ in) in k3 p3 rib in rows. Then increase 1 st in first and last sts of each group of knit sts (= k5 p3). Work until collar measures 14 cm (5½ in). Repeat the increases (= k7, p3). Work until collar measures 18 cm (7 in). On last row, work a 'knot' in 2nd and 6th sts of each group of knit sts.
**Knot:** Work 5 sts in 1 st (alternately k1

and k1tbl). Work 5 rows st st over these 5 sts. Work these 5 sts together (by slipping the sts one by one over the 1st stitch). Cast off.

## Loose sleeves:

Beginning at the top, cast on 42 sts. Work 1 rd k, 1 rd p, 1 rd k, 1 rd p (= 2 ridges). Work 24 cm (9½ in) st st. Place a marker at the centre underarm. Continue in st st, shaping the elbow as follows: work until 2 sts past the marker and turn. Work until 2 sts past marker (on wrong side) and turn. Continue in the same way, always working 2 extra sts on each side, until there are 20 sts between the turns. Then work 2 sts less on each round until there are only 4 sts between the turns. Work 3 cm (1¼ in) in st st in rounds. Place a marker at the centre of the opposite side of the sleeve from the elbow. Cast off 1 st at each side of marker every 4th rd 6 times (= 30 sts). Work 2 ridges garter st. Then work 6 rds in k3, p3 rib increasing in knit sts, working 'knots' on the last row as described for the poncho collar in 2nd and 6th st of each group of plain sts. Cast off.
Felt as described on page 4, but at 30°C.

# Turquoise heart sweater

Pretty V-neck sweater with raglan sleeves. The right sleeve has a heart in a hole pattern on the shoulder.

**Size:** S – M – L – XL

**Yarn: pt2** (or **Rauma Finullgarn**)
Turquoise 24 (6024)      5 – 5 – 6 – 6 balls

**Measurements:**
Bust: 90 – 95 – 100 – 105 cm (35½ – 37½ – 39½ – 41½ in)
Overall length: 49 – 53 – 56 – 60 cm (19½ – 21 – 22¼ – 23¾ in)
Sleeve length: 43 – 44 – 45 – 46 cm (17 – 17½ – 17¾ – 18¼ in)

**Suggested needles:** Circular needle and set of 5 double-pointed needles size 5 mm. Crochet hook size 3 mm.

**Tension:**
**Before felting:** Approx 15 sts st st = 10 cm (4 in)
**After felting:** Approx 16 sts = 10 cm (4 in)

## Body:

Cast on 144 – 152 – 160 – 168 sts. Join into ring, work 20 rds st st. Place a marker at each side with 72 – 76 – 80 – 84 sts for back and front. Decrease 1 st each side of markers on every 10th rd twice. NB: For the front, begin the pattern in chart A on the first decrease round. Start 10 cm (4 in) from the side marker. Work until body measures 36 – 38 – 40 – 42 cm (14¼ – 15 – 16 – 16½ in). Cast off 6 sts at each side for armhole (= 3 sts either side of markers). Lay the work aside and knit sleeves.

## Sleeves:

Cast on 50 – 52 – 54 – 56 sts. Work 43 – 44 – 45 – 46 cm (17 – 17½ – 17¾ – 18¼ in) st st in rounds. Cast off 6 sts at centre underarm.

## Joining the pieces:

Slip the body and arms on to a circular needle = 212 – 224 – 236 – 248 sts, placing markers at the 4 places where the body and sleeves meet. Decrease 1 st on each side of each marker on every alternate row as follows: Work k2togtbl before the marker and k2tog after the marker (= 8 sts decreased on row). At the same time as decreasing for raglan, decrease for the V-neck as follows: Beginning at centre front and working in rows, decrease 1 st at neck edge (1 st inside edge st) every 4th row once, then every alternate row. At the right side of the front, decrease by working k1, k2togtbl. At the left side, work k2tog, k1 at end of row. NB: On the same row as the 3rd raglan decrease, begin working the pattern shown in chart B, at the centre of the right shoulder. Continue decreasing for neck and raglan until all sts on the front have been cast off. Cast off the remaining sts. Crochet around all edges as follows: 1 dc, 8 ch, *miss 3, 8ch, 1dc in next st*, rep from * to *.

Felt lightly in washing machine on a short programme at 30°C.
See also page 8.

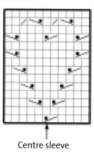

Chart B

Centre sleeve

Chart A

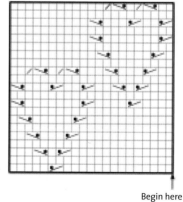

Begin here

☐ = k
▱ = k2tog, yfd
◺ = yfd, s1, k1, psso
▱ = yfd, s1, k2tog, psso, yfd

# Easter Basket

We used paint to colour the lace on this basket, but of course you could use fabric dye instead. You could also trim it with other Easter decorations. The possibilities are endless.

**Yarn: Røros Lamullgarn**
White L11          1 ball

**Suggestions for trimming:**
50 cm (20 in) yellow lace (white lace can be dyed with fabric dye). If you wish to line the basket, you will need 20 cm (8 in) fabric in a matching colour and iron-on interfacing.

**Measurements:** Approx 14 cm (5⅝ in) diameter

**Suggested needles:** Short circular needle 40cm (16in) size 4 mm

**Tension:**
**Before felting:** Approx 18 sts st st = 10 cm (4 in)
**After felting:** Approx 22 sts = 10 cm (4 in)

Cast on 80 sts. Work 45 rounds st st. Then knit the row of holes by repeating *k2tog, yfd* to end of row. Work 2 rds st st. Next round: decrease by working *k6, k2tog*, rep to end. Work 2 rds st st. Next round: decrease by working *k5, k2tog*, rep to end. Continue decreasing on every 3rd rd, with 1 less st between decreases each time until 10 sts remain. Cut the yarn and pull through sts.
Felt as described on page 8.
Cut a circle of card/cardboard the size of the basket (measure the diameter to be on the safe side). Place this in the bottom. Measure the circumference of the basket, and cut corrugated card to fit. Tape the ends together and place it inside the basket. Leave it there until the basket is completely dry.

Fold about 2.5cm (1 in) over to the outside. Sew the lace round the edge. The basket could well be lined. Use the pieces you cut out of cardboard as a pattern, cutting off the top 3 cm (1¼ in). Add 1cm (⅜ in) along all sides. Cut out two pieces for the bottom and two for the sides. Iron interfacing on one bottom and one side piece. Sew the short edges of the side piece together and sew to the bottom. With right sides together, sew the lining to the basket at the top, leaving a small opening for turning the work right side out. Sew up the opening by hand.

# Yellow mat

Practical mat crocheted in double yarn.

**Yarn: Rauma Finullgarn (or pt2)**
Yellow 450 (75)     1 ball
Green 455 (15)     1 ball
**Measurements:** Approx 20 cm (8 in) diameter
**Suggested needle:** Crochet hook size 6.5 mm
Using yellow yarn double, work 8ch and join in a ring with 1ss in 1st ch.
**Round 1:** 2 ch (= first tr), 11 more tr in ring, finish with 1 ss in first tr.
**Round 2:** 2 ch (= first tr) + 1 tr in first tr, 2 tr in each of the next 11 tr, finish with 1 ss in first tr.

**Round 3:** 2 ch(= first tr), 2 tr in next tr, *1 tr in next tr, 2 tr in next tr*, rep from * to * and finish with 1 ss in first tr.
**Round 4:** 2 ch (= first tr), 1 tr in next tr, 2 tr in next tr, *1 tr in each of the next 2 tr, 2 tr in next tr*, rep from * to * and finish with 1 ss in first tr.
**Round 5:** 2 ch (= first tr), 1 tr in each of the next 2 tr, 2 tr in next tr, *1 tr in each of the next 3 tr, 2 tr in next tr*, rep from * to * and finish with 1 ss in first tr.
**Round 6:** 2 ch (= first tr), 1 tr in each of the next 3 tr, 2 tr in next tr, *1 tr in each of the next 4 tr, 2 tr in next tr*,

rep from * to * and finish with 1 ss in first tr. Cut the yarn.
**Round 7:** With green yarn used double, work 1 ss in first tr, 1 ss in each of the next 4 tr, 2 ss in next tr, *1 ss in each of the next 5 tr, 2 ss in next tr*, rep from * to * and finish with 1 ss in first tr.
Felt as described on page 8.

# Slippers for all the family

Slippers for ladies and girls inspired by indoor shoes, and 'filled-in' slippers for boys and men.

## Girls' and ladies' slippers

**Sizes:**
Children's sizes:
20–22, 24–26, 28–30 (5–6, 7–8, 10–11)
Adults' sizes:
32–34, 36–38, 40–42 (1–2, 4–5, 7–8)
**Yarn:** Rauma Finullgarn (or **pt2**)
**Blue slippers:**

| | |
|---|---|
| **Colour 1:** Blue 472 (32) | 1–2 balls |
| **Colour 2:** Pink 465 (54) | 1 ball |
| **Colour 3:** Pale pink 479 (55) | 1 ball |
| **Colour 4:** Green 493 (17) | 1 ball |
| **Colour 5:** Lime 454 (14) | 1 ball |

**White slippers:**

**Colour 1:** White 401 (0)          1–2 balls
**Suggested trimmings:** 6 pastel pink satin flowers

**Pink slippers:**
**Colour 1:** Pink 479 (55)          1–2 balls
**Suggested trimmings:** 2 red satin flowers

**Suggested needles:** Short circular needle 40cm (16in) and set of 5 double-pointed needles size 5mm. Crochet hook

**Tension:**
**Before felting:** Approx 16 sts st st = 10 cm (4 in)
**After felting:** Approx 20 sts = 10 cm (4 in)

Pattern continues on page 72

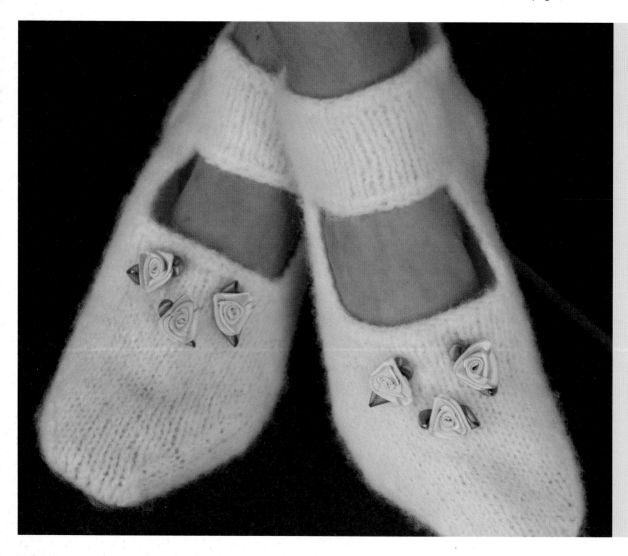

With colour 1, cast on 32 – 36 – 40 – 44 – 46 – 50 sts. Work 10 – 10 – 12 – 12 – 14 – 14 rds st st. Next round: cast off 8 – 10 – 10 – 12 – 13 – 15 sts in the middle of the top of the foot (have the beginning of the round at centre back). Slip 4 – 4 – 5 – 5 – 5 – 5 sts at each side of the cast-off sts onto threads. Work the heel on the remaining 16 – 18 – 20 – 22 – 23 – 25 sts as follows: Work until there is 1 st remaining at one side, turn, and work until there is 1 st remaining at the other side. Turn and work until there are 2 sts remaining at one side, turn, and work until there are 2 sts remaining at the other side. Continue in the same way until there are 4 – 4 – 6 – 6 – 7 – 7 sts remaining at centre. Then work 1 st more at each side until all the heel sts have been knitted again. Slip the sts from the thread back on to the needle = 24 – 26 – 30 – 32 – 33 – 35 sts. Work 8 – 10 – 12 – 14 – 16 – 18 rows. Cast on 8 – 10 – 10 – 12 – 13 – 15 sts in the middle of the top of the foot = 32 – 36 – 40 – 44 – 46 – 50 sts. Work 12 – 14 – 16 – 18 – 20 – 22 rounds. Place a marker at each side, with 16 – 18 – 20 – 22 – 23 – 25 sts on top of foot and the same number underneath. Decrease 1 st at each side of markers, with 2 sts in between, on every alternate round until 12 – 12 – 16 – 16 – 18 – 18 sts remain. Graft together. Crochet dc around the edges (1 dc in each st).

**Blue slippers:** Embroider the design as shown in the photo. Start with stem stitch to mark the leaves and petals. In the centre of the flower, embroider French knots, wrapping the yarn 4 times round the needle.

**White and pink slippers:** Trim with satin flowers (see photo).

# Boys' and men's slippers:

**Sizes:**
Children's sizes:
20–22, 24–26, 28–30 (5–6, 7–8, 10–11)
Adults' sizes:
32–34, 36–38, 40–42, 44–46 (1–2, 4–5, 7–8, 10–11)
**Yarn: Rauma Finullgarn (or pt2)**
Light brown 406 (79)          1–2 balls

**Suggested needles:** Short circular needle 40cm (16in) and set of 5 double-pointed needles size 5mm. Crochet hook
**Tension:**
**Before felting:** Approx 16 sts st st = 10 cm (4 in)
**After felting:** Approx 20 sts = 10 cm (4 in)
Cast on 32 – 36 – 40 – 44 – 46 – 50 – 52 sts. Work 14 – 14 – 16 – 18 – 18 – 20 – 20 rds st st. Now work heel over the 16 – 18 – 20 – 22 – 23 – 25 –26 sts at centre back (have the beginning of the round at centre back). Work until there is 1 st remaining at one side, turn, and work until there is 1 st remaining at the other side. Turn and work until there are 2 sts remaining at

one side, turn, and work until there are 2 sts remaining at the other side. Continue in the same way until there are 4 – 4 – 6 – 6 – 7 – 7 – 8 sts remaining at centre. Then work 1 st more at each side until all the heel sts have been knitted again. Work 20 – 24 – 28 – 32 – 36 – 40 – 42 rounds. Place a marker at each side, with 16 – 18 – 20 – 22 – 23 – 25 – 26 sts on top of foot and the same number underneath. Decrease 1 st at each side of markers, with 2 sts in between, on every alternate round until 12 – 12 – 16 – 16 – 18 – 18 – 20 sts remain. Graft together. Crochet dc around the edges (1dc in each st).
Felt as described on page 8.

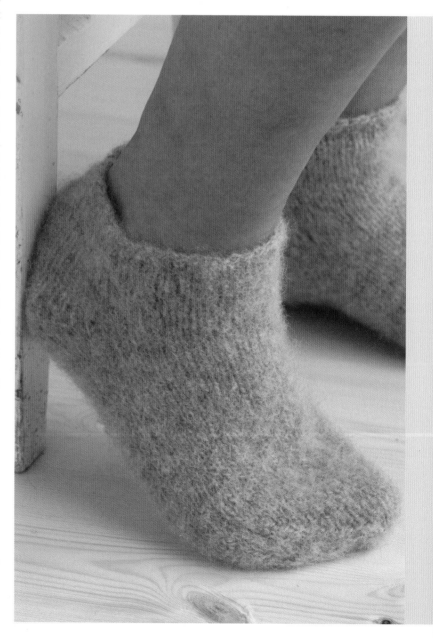

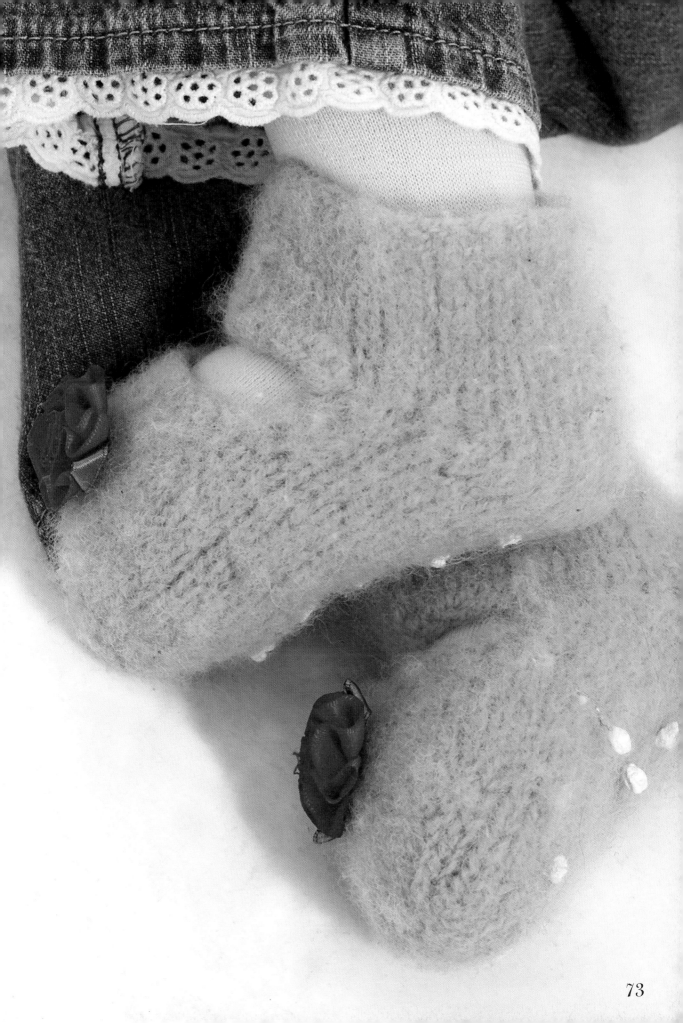

# Funky hat, mittens and slippers

The hat and mittens are worked in stocking stitch, and the slippers in garter stitch.

**Size:** Ladies'
**Yarn: pt2** (or **Rauma Finullgarn**)
Orange 72 (460)   4 balls
Pink 54 (465)     2 ball
Lime 16 (454)     1 ball

**Measurements:**
Shape the slippers to fit the foot and the mittens to the hand. Shape the hat by trying it on.

**Suggested needles:** Circular needle and set of 5 double-pointed needles size 5mm

**Tension:**
**Before felting:** Approx 16 sts st st = 10cm (4in)
**After felting:** Approx 20 sts = 10cm (4in)
**Before felting:** Approx 14 sts garter st = 10cm (4in)
**After felting:** Approx 18 sts = 10cm (4in)

## Hat:

Begin at the bottom of one ear-flap. With orange, cast on 5 sts. Work in st st in rows, increasing 1 st at each side on every alternate row until there are 29 sts on needle. Cut the yarn. Knit the second flap in the same way. Begin the hat at the centre back by casting on 8 sts. Knit across 1 flap. Cast on 46 sts, knit across the second flap and cast on 8 sts = 120 sts. Work 23cm (9in) in st st in rounds. Next round: decrease by working *k6, k2tog*, rep to end of rd. Work 5 rds. Next round: *k5, k2tog*, rep to end of rd. Work 5 rds. Next round: *k4, k2tog*, rep to end of rd. Continue decreasing, but now on every 4th rd, with 1 less st between decreases each time, until 30 sts remain.

Next 2 rounds: *k2, k2tog*, rep to end. Cut the yarn and thread through sts.
**Fringes:** Cut 12cm (4¾in) lengths of orange yarn. Use three strands for each tassel. Attach the tassels close together, about 1cm (⅜in) from the edge (pulling them through the threads of 2 stitches) and leave sts on thread.

## Mittens:

Make the mittens with the following colour sequences:
**Mitten 1:** Work 7cm (2¾in) in orange, 5cm (2in) in lime, 13cm (5¼in) in pink, 4cm (1¾in) in orange and the rest in lime. Work the thumb in pink.
**Mitten 2:** Work 7cm (2¾in) in orange, 4cm (1¾in) in pink, 14cm (5½in) in lime, and the rest in orange. Work the thumb in lime.

**Make the mittens as follows:**
With orange yarn, cast on 62 sts. Join into a ring. Work in st st in rounds, decreasing 4 sts evenly spaced on every 8th rd 3 times = 46 sts. Continue straight until work measures 13cm (5¼in). Next round: for the thumb gusset, increase 1 st on each side of the first stitch of the round. Work 4 rds. Next round: increase 1 st each side of the stitches you increased previously. Increase in the same way on every 5th rd, so that each time there are 2 more sts between the sts you increased in, until there are 9 sts in the gusset (54 sts on needle). Continue until work measures 22cm (8¾in). Slip the 9 sts of the gusset on to a thread. Cast on 9 sts over these and work 11cm (4½in) in rounds. Next round: decrease 6 sts evenly spaced. Work 6 rds without shaping. Next round: decrease 6 sts evenly spaced. Work 5 rds without shaping. Continue decreasing 6 sts over the round, with 1 rd less between decreases each time, until 12 sts remain. Work 1 rd without shaping. Next round: k2tog to end of rd = 6 sts. Cut the yarn and pull through sts.

**Thumb:** Slip the sts from the thread on to a needle. Pick up and knit the 9 cast-on sts + 1 st at each side = 20 sts. Work 7 cm (2¾ in) st st in rounds. Next round: decrease 4 sts evenly spaced. Work 3 rds without shaping. Next round: decrease 4 sts evenly spaced. Work 2 rds without shaping. Next round: decrease 4 sts evenly spaced. Cut the yarn and thread it through the sts.

**Fringes:** Cut 12 cm (4¾ in) lengths of orange yarn. Use three strands for each tassel. Attach the tassels close together, about 1 cm (⅜ in) from the edge (pulling them through the threads of 2 stitches).

## Slippers:

Work in the following colour sequence: 10 'ridges' in orange, 10 ridges in lime, and the rest in pink.

The slippers are worked in garter stitch in rows, using double yarn.

Begin at the top of the ankle. Cast on 48 sts loosely. Work 23 ridges (= 46 rows) garter st. Cast off 17 sts loosely at each side. Work 19 ridges on the remaining 14 sts (= sole). Cut the yarn (but leave sts on needle). Pick up 1 st at each side of the bottom 14 ridges of the ankle. Slip these sts on to the needle on each side of the

stitches of the sole (= 42 sts). Work 16 ridges. Next row: decrease 6 sts evenly spaced. Repeat decrease row, working 5 rows in between once, 3 rows once and 1 row twice. Next row: k2tog to end of row. Cut the yarn and pull through sts. Sew the ankle and the top of the foot together with double yarn and loose stitches. Sew together at each side of the sole and heel.

**Fringes:** Cut 12 cm (4 in) lengths of orange yarn. Use three strands for each tassel. Attach the tassels close together, 1 ridge below the cast-on edge.

Felt the items as described on page 8.

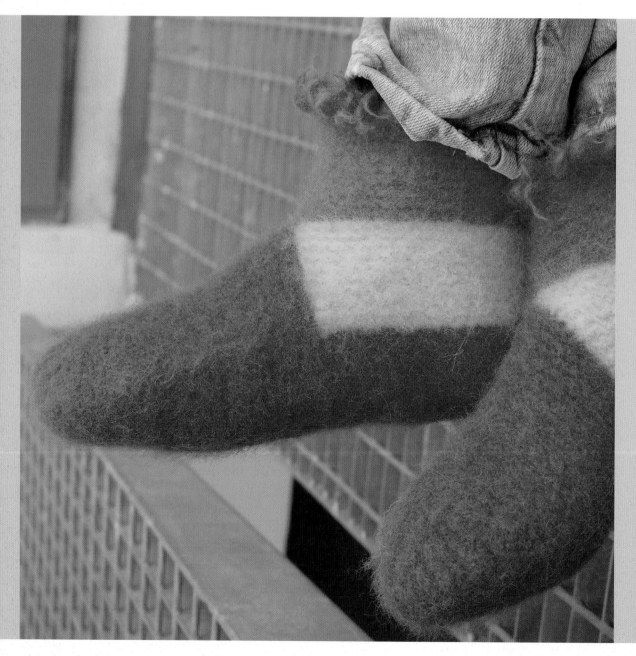

A sitting man does not need honour,

he needs warm stockings.

Knut Hamsun

Nordic Felted Knits

First published in Great Britain
2007 by Search Press Limited
Originally published in Norway
2006 by Kom Forlag AS

Project Manager:
Kirsti Kielland Gran

Chief designer:
Gerd Fjellanger

Other designers:
Berit Wollebæk Kristoffersen,
Pages 32, 44, 58, 74.
Bodil Svanemyr, page 16.
Hildegard Digernes, page 66.
Birte Aartun, page 60.
Britt Aasen Brude, page 64

Chief photographer:
Espen Grønli

Other photographers:
Lars Crone, pages 37, 44, 61, 66.
Ragnar Hartvig, page 33.
Pt foto, pages 64, 65, 74, 75, 76.
Petter Berg, pages 27, 29.
Fotograferne Sima, pages 8, 22,
23, 35, 73.

Graphic design:
Talén | Jakobsen

English edition typeset by
GreenGate Publishing Services,
Tonbridge, Kent

Printed by Nørhaven

ISBN-10: 1-84448-255-3
ISBN-13: 978-1-84448-255-9